BRISTOL:
The Growing City

LIFE IN THE SUBURBS
FROM THE 18TH CENTURY
TO TODAY

James Belsey
•
David Harrison
•
Martin Powell
•
Helen Reid
•
Pat Smith

Published in association with
Bristol & West Building Society

1804614427

REDCLIFFE
Bristol

First published in 1986 by
Redcliffe Press Ltd, 49 Park Street, Bristol 1
in association with Bristol & West Building Society.

ISBN 0 948265 95 7

*Typeset and printed in Great Britain by
Penwell Ltd, Parkwood, Callington, Cornwall*

CONTENTS

Front Cover: East Street, Bedminster

West Town Lane: Brislington as a village.

Introduction

Probably the most surprising fact that the casual delver in Bristol's history discovers is just how small the city was until just over a century ago.

The original Bristol was, of course, little bigger than the current Broadmead shopping centre, but the city was still surrounded by walls at the beginning of the 18th century.

The only way in was through the ancient gates of Redcliff, Temple, Newgate and the other sites easily traceable in today's street names. Only St John's Gate still survives from the six. The old city was surrounded then by small villages and hamlets, most of which were to be swallowed in the following centuries as Bristol spread in all directions. To the west growth was stopped by the Avon Gorge: to the south, the Dundry slopes provided a natural barrier. In the north and east, the new motorways form a man-made boundary to keep development out of further rural areas.

Not all of what appears on the map as a city mass is Bristol. The remorseless spread of housing and factories, the infilling of gaps, the need for new homes and employment for those forced from the city centre by slum clearance or German bombs have led to a city that crosses several local government boundaries. Kingswood, for instance, has its own council but, without road signs, who could say where Bristol now ends and Kingswood begins?

Just look back across the centuries to the beginning of the 18th century. John Latimer, journalist and local historian, provided an evocative picture of Bristol as it then was, little changed from medieval times except for new housing on the site of the old castle.

"Saving half a dozen houses edging on what is now called Park Row—then the only carriage road to Clifton—and a few cottages in Frog Lane, the slope of ground extending from the Royal Fort to the harbour, was occupied by orchards, fields and gardens", he wrote.

"Stokes Croft was a rural promenade, having fields on either side and was sheltered from the summer sun by rows of trees. Kingsdown was literally a down, ramblers on which beheld a grove of church steeples on the one hand and stretches of pasture lands and orchards on the other. More to the West, the city ended near St Michael's Church and at College Green.

"Clifton, on the hill, was divided by about a dozen dairy farms, separated here and there by unenclosed common, gay with furze blossom. A single mansion, the Manor House, stood near the church and another in Clifton Wood. Around them straggled a few cottages, the inmates of which earned a little money from the parish by killing the foxes, polecats and hedgehogs that strayed from the downs into the cultivated fields.

"Even in the low-lying district, although a few lodging houses had sprung up for the accommodation of visitors to the Hot Well, the road from College Green, until far into the century, ran between gardens, dotted at intervals by houses.

"Bedminster was even more isolated than Clifton . . . a clear space of half a mile separated the city from the village. Redcliff and Temple Gates looked upon open country as late as 1730. In fact, Bristol had only one real suburb—the district lying beyond Lawford's Gate, inhabited by a few hundred weavers, colliers and market gardeners."

By 1800, Clifton, Cotham and Redland and all the growing eastern suburbs were still outside the city boundaries and were complaining bitterly about the lack of street lights or night constables. A century later, it was the city which was feeling annoyed by the move to the suburbs of thousands of Bristolians who, as Latimer put it, were "enjoying all the benefits of the city whilst escaping its burdens and responsibilities."

In 1891, the city tried to take over Horfield, Stapleton, St George, part of Mangotsfield, Oldland, Hanham, part of Brislington, part of Bedminster, part of Long Ashton, Shirehampton, part of Henbury and part of Westbury. More than 72,300 people lived in these parishes and the rateable value was a healthy £270,000. The parishioners rejected the takeover, and with further opposition from the Gloucestershire and Somerset county councils, the matter was dropped.

In 1894, Bristol tried again, this time with a Parliamentary Bill, which proposed absorbing the parishes of Horfield, Stapleton, Shirehampton, St George and Kingswood and the urban sections of Westbury, Mangotsfield, Brislington, Bedminster and Long Ashton. Bristol also wanted a small portion of Henbury, and Dunball Island, a minor fragment of Easton-in-Gordano which had become detached by a change in the course of the River Avon.

There was bitter opposition from Gloucestershire and Somerset, the inhabitants of most of the parishes affected and, for some obscure reason, both the railway companies and the Corporation of the Poor. Latimer puts his finger on it as usual when he comments drily: "The unwillingness of many wealthy residents in Stoke Bishop, Sneyd Park and Leigh Woods—the majority of them Bristolians—to be made liable to city taxation, was the most prominent feature of the opposition."

To Bristol's chagrin, a Parliamentary select committee agreed the city could have all the poorer areas including Avonmouth dock and village, but not the richer parts like Westbury and Henbury. In 1896, there was a third try, aimed at a smaller area in the wealthy north west, but a bigger one around Brislington. The Duke of Beaufort and the inhabitants of Horfield, Stapleton, Sneyd Park and Stoke Bishop again fought the measure and again Bristol's proposals were accepted—with the exception of Sneyd Park, Stoke Bishop and northern Horfield! The new boundaries meant Bristol now covered nearly 11,500 acres.

The following year, a Home Office Commissioner recommended the formation of wards in the areas newly within the city boundaries. These were Somerset, Stapleton, Easton, St George and Horfield and were each represented by three councillors and an alderman.

In 1900, there was a formal "perambulation of the city boundaries", a move considered essential to persuade rebellious new Bristolians that they were now living in the city.

It lasted a fortnight by foot, carriage and steamer, starting from the bottom of St Vincents Rocks, Clifton and proceeding up on to the Downs, along to Parry's Lane and around the edge of Westbury to Horfield. "In that neighbourhood," says Latimer, "various houses standing across the boundary line had to be passed through, or surmounted, by means of ladders."

On across Purdown, for a courtesy call on the Dowager Duchess of Beaufort at Stoke House, "where the Lord High Steward and the Lord Mayor underwent a process of bumping which had already been undergone by most of the pedestrians, several ladies and a baby".

Frenchay was next; along the Frome to Downend and Staple Hill and thence to Kingswood and Kingswood Chase. Here again, the boundary line had been drawn through houses and factories which once more involved much scrambling over walls and through homes.

From Magpie Bottom, the walk became hard going with water-cress beds, marshes, orchards and gardens, but the remaining walkers were met at Conham for a steamer trip to Hanham weir before continuing to Brislington and St Annes. Bedminster, Bedminster Down, Bishopsworth and Rownham completed the perambulation which by this time had become less than dignified with a volunteer bumping corps formed by a party of young women who dealt vigorously with many of the walkers.

On the fifteenth and final day, 250 people boarded the steamer Brittania to survey the water boundaries, landing at Shirehampton and Portishead to fix the line between Bristol, and Gloucestershire and Somerset respectively. Iron stakes were also driven into Steep Holm and Flat Holm to mark Bristol's claim there.

Bristol was to expand further in the following 80 years but most of the acquisitions were sensible infilling and the absorption of villages which were no longer separate units. It didn't stop the vociferous opposition and even today some people in Westbury-on-Trym, Coombe Dingle and Shirehampton like to think of themselves as communities apart from the vulgar city.

Bristol may expand again before the end of the century for most of the new hi-tech industries moving to the area are outside the city limits in Northavon—but in an area bounded by the motorways and vulnerable to boundary changes. In the meantime, this book is an affectionate look at how Bristol's suburbs grew and changed; how little villages became swallowed up to the extent that little but the name remains. It is a book drawn from old records, crumbling newspapers, the tireless and numerous local historians that Bristol has produced and, most of all, from the memories of the inhabitants.

David Harrison
September 1986

Up on the Hill

Helen Reid examines the fall of a Bristol Spa while the city rises to new heights.

Most histories of Hotwells and Clifton begin with the 18th century development of the area as a spa. But the story should begin a century earlier.

It is not conceivable that the whole economy of the two suburbs rested entirely on the waters of the Hot Well. Though no traces of any buildings earlier than the 18th century remain in Hotwells, there must have been earlier settlement, because of its position on the earliest crossing of the Avon, at Rownham and at the entrance to the Bristol Docks, and there is plenty of proof that throughout the 17th century, Hotwells was an industrialised area. Clifton at the time was a district of farms and common land, and had only one manor house. Clifton Wood, which was literally the wood of Clifton manor, was let out to lime-burners who produced mortar for the building boom in central Bristol. "Tennyments" were built for the lime-kiln workers, along the Clifton Wood slopes and on the Hotwell Road, and because of the large lime production, and the glass-house at the foot of Brandon Hill, on Limekiln Dock, the area became the centre of the building trade, and remained so throughout the 18th century. St George's Road was until the 1860's known as Limekiln Lane, and housed dozens of carpenters, glaziers, painters, and in the 1790's, famous figures such as William Paty, the architect, and Thomas Stocking, the plasterer.

So when the Hot Well became fashionable, from 1700 onwards, the building boom it created was made possible by the fact that the materials and the workers were already established in the area.

The virtues of the Hot Well waters were known in the 17th century—they were believed to be a cure for leprosy—but the spa did not get organised until 1696 when the spring was enclosed and the first Pump House was built. Following the example of Bath, the Hot Well became a social as well as a medical centre; the fashionable and famous flocked there to drink the water which Alexander Pope described as "brisk and soft on the palate, grateful to the stomach and wholly free from odour. It was full and warm as new milk from the cow." Such was the fame of the water that it was sold in London (it was sent by sea in Bristol-made bottles) and exported to the West Indies. Unlike the water of Bath, it did not deteriorate in the bottle.

Knowing modern Hotwells, it is hard to imagine the place as the great social centre it became in the 18th century. Carriages ran regularly from the city, for a sixpenny fare, and in the season, which lasted from April to September, shop-keepers from London and Bath would set up branches. At the Long Room, facing the water, there were society breakfasts, balls, card-playing, plays (Gay's *Beggar's Opera* had 50 performances there in 1728) and concerts, and at night, boats would take parties down the Avon, with a band and fireworks and a cold collation. There was a pleasure garden, several hotels, and in 1754 Elizabeth Trinder, the noted Bath cook, opened her dining rooms, where she sold the first ever recorded set lunches, at half a crown a head. Her restaurant was at the Lebeck, a large house in Chapel Row, demolished in the 1950's when it was an appalling slum housing 38 families who lived there without gas or electricity.

Dowry Square, built from 1727, was the focus of early Hotwell society, and these houses were clearly built speculatively for lodging houses. The largest, with the dovecote (no. 9) was advertised in 1748 as being "built on purpose for lodgings, having below stairs two large kitchens and servants' hall, laundry, cellars, pantries, both sorts of water (i.e. drinking and non-drinking) and all other conveniences." Albemarle Row (1768) was built for the same purpose, and lack of accommodation was a permanent problem. "Every fine Sunday the place is like a fair, vast numbers coming from Bristol and all round to drink the water," wrote an observer in 1754. Plainly expansion up the hill and into Clifton was necessary.

In 1750, there were only a handful of fine houses in Clifton, on the Green, where Thomas Goldney had built his mansion, and bought back some of the lime-kiln land for his estate. The urgent need was for lodging houses for the Hotwell patrons who wanted to take the Clifton air, botanise, ride on the Downs and admire the Gorge, which since Elizabethan times, had been famous for its scenery and as a breeding ground for hawks.

So the building boom began, and it is ironic to note that what are considered now to be the best properties in Clifton—Sion Hill, West Mall, Royal York Crescent—were originally just lodging houses. Moreover they remained lodgings for most of their history, until the post World War II gentrification.

But the Clifton building boom really got going too late. For after 1790, the popularity of the Hot Well declined rapidly, for various reasons. The main one was that the Merchant Venturers who owned the site, required the new lessee in 1784 to pay more rent and make expensive improvements. This led to much higher charges, and the visitors who had just come for social reasons stayed away, leaving the spa to the invalids. Since medical knowledge was increasing, and doctors were less convinced of the cure-all properties of the water, only desperate cases came to the Hot Well, and their inevitable deaths were a poor advertisement. Mary Morton's father put this poignant memorial to her in Bristol Cathedral: "To Bristol's fount I bore with trembling care her faded form. She bowed to taste the healing wave and died." She was 28. Another reads: "The

Top: Clifton Suspension Bridge under construction. Two noted nineteenth century rendez-vous face each other across the water: the Spring tea gardens and the Hotwells spa. **Bottom:** Later in the century. The Favell, owned and built by Charles Hill & Sons.

healing spring no more could lend its aid.''

Andrew Carrick, a Clifton physician who observed the rise and fall of the Hot Well, wrote a book on the subject in 1816, in which he described how the patients, mainly consumptives, arrived: ''One consumptive from Scotland expired just as the carriage which brought him reached the door of his lodgings. Another died within the week, and several did not live to reach the end of their journey.'' There were so many deaths that one row of lodgings became known as Death Row. ''From the day that the Hot Well became a fountain sealed to the lips of everyone but the actually moribund, the fame of the place began rapidly to decline. None who drank of the Lethean waters were thenceforth found to recover, because none did drink of it but such as were past recovery,'' says Carrick. ''It was now one uniform black list of disappointment and death, and in the course of a very few years, it became all over the kingdom a source of horror and despair, instead of joy and confidence, to be ordered to the Hot Well, from whose bourne no traveller returned.''

Carrick also attributed the deaths to the insanitary houses, which having no wallpaper (which cost 10s to 13s a yard then) were a damp breeding place for germs.

And this was the very period when the major building projects started in Clifton. The decline of the Hot Well, coupled with the slump caused by the Napoleonic Wars, meant bankruptcy for the builders of Windsor Terrace, Royal York Crescent and Boyce's Buildings, many of which remained uncompleted until as late as 1815. Around the turn of the century it was estimated that as many as 500 houses lay unfinished in Clifton.

What is surprising is that the spa movement went on for so long. The second Hot Well Pump House was not demolished until 1867; the water was still drunk by locals, and there was a brief revival of life at Hotwells when the steamships from all over the West Coast came in daily. Hot Well water was still being bottled and sold as late as 1851: James Bolton advertised his ''mineral aerated waters, lemonade etc., made from the celebrated Hotwell water.'' By this time, Clifton was being promoted as a resort, famous for its air, its flora (the area at the junction of Pembroke Road and Queens Road was known as Flower Hill) and above all, for the Avon Gorge which became a new focus of interest from 1862 onwards, when the Suspension Bridge was started. Long before then, in the 17th and 18th centuries, the Gorge attracted extravagant praise, in terms which it is hard for us to understand.

The view is spectacular, but John Evelyn, for example, writing in 1654, talked of ''the precipice which is equal to anything of that nature which I have seen in the more confragose (rugged and broken) cataracts of the Alps.''

Morgan's 1851 guide speaks of ''highly romantic and picturesque

Lebeck House, Dowry Parade: 'dozens of poor families lived here'. Demolished in 1964 for new flats.

views and declivites of rocks'' and added: "The man of taste would ever gaze on it with rapture and astonishment." We can only conclude that the Gorge looked rather different then; subsequent widening and straightening of the river banks, the building of the Portway and incessant quarrying have smoothed out the contours and tamed the drama that so impressed the 19th century Bristol school of artists, and poets Wordsworth and Coleridge.

The first person to cross the Suspension Bridge on 9 December 1864, was 21 year old Mary Griffiths of Hanham. And by an astonishing spanning of the centuries, we know all about her feat because she made a broadcast about it, at the age of 93, in 1936.

She went with her uncle to the Clifton side. "I was determined to get as near and to see as much as I could," she told listeners to the BBC. "So I pushed up to the front and got right up to the gate that had been erected across the entrance to the bridge. When the signal was given and the gate was opened, I suddenly decided to be the first across, so I began to run.

"I had not run very far when I heard my uncle shout 'Run, Mary, run' and I turned round and saw a young man some yards behind me, running as fast as he could. I could see he was trying to beat me across, and I tucked up my long dress and ran for dear life—and I beat him by a few yards! When I came back, my uncle was very pleased and said, 'Well, you did it, Mary!' and I had. I remember it as if it were only yesterday."

Mrs Griffiths also remembered another incident. "At the time of the opening ceremony a hotel was being built somewhere near the Clifton entrance and the scaffolding was being used by a number of people as a grandstand. I am not sure whether it was the day of the official opening ceremony or the day after, but I do remember that a portion of the scaffolding collapsed, throwing a number of women into the roadway some distance below. I believe some of them were seriously injured."

From the 1860's there was drama of another kind, the Suspension Bridge, as historian John Latimer observed, seemed to possess "an irresistible attraction to persons afflicted with suicidal derangement." The first suicide took place in May 1866.

But the water story was not over in Clifton, for the domestic water supply was a vexed question. Hotwells water was used as drinking and domestic water by those nearby; in Clifton they had to rely on wells and springs which were privately owned. During a drought, as in 1864, householders would hire carriages, and tour the district with an empty barrel, trying to buy water. There was a fine spring at Sion House (next to St Vincent's Rocks Hotel) which produced 33,560 gallons a day, and fed a bath-house, and the owner sold water to local residents at a penny a barrel; the iron traps still visible in the road in Caledonia Place gave access to cisterns which

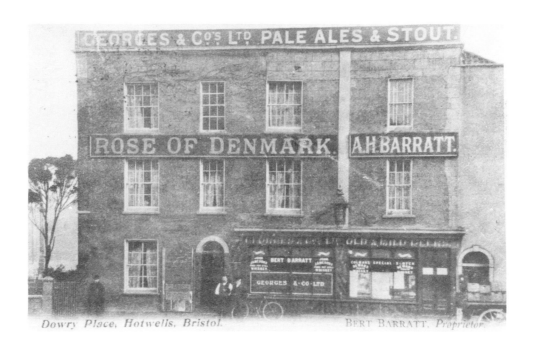

Dowry Place, Hotwells, Bristol.   BERT BARRATT, *Proprietor.*

Two of Hotwells' many public houses.

were filled from the Sion Spring, and in 1845 the owner was selling water to 304 houses.

There were other springs at Grosvenor Place (the Richmond Springs pub site) and at Buckingham Vale; Hotwells also used a spring on the Mardyke, or the water from Jacob's Well, which since medieval times had supplied the area and College Green. Nothing came of the Merchant Venturers' plan to pump the Hot Well water up to a huge reservoir on Observatory Hill, and in the end Bristol Waterworks bought up the private springs for around £21,000. And so died one ambitious scheme to heat the houses in the Richmond Terrace area with hot spring water in pipes.

But the spa story does not even end there: the last gasp came when the Grand Spa Hydro opened in 1894, using water pumped up from the Hot Well. The building had been allowed on condition that the developer built the Clifton Rocks Railway as well. But the elaborate Pump Room, with its baths and fountains, was never a great success and it later became a cinema and then a ballroom. It now lies decaying under the road opposite Caledonia Place. The water saga finally ends in 1913, when the Hot Well spring, pumped up to a cave still visible on the Hotwell Road, just beyond the Colonnade, was sealed because of the fears of pollution. Even in 1913, a few hundred people a day were still drinking the water, which by then was no longer as hot, (and probably not even chemically the same) as the original water. We shall never know what it tasted like, because attempts in 1913 and 1925 to find the original source failed. Nor will we ever know exactly what its curative properties were: it is likely that there was a placebo effect, judging from John Wesley's comment in 1754. He supplemented the doctor's directions to drink the water with "a plaster of brimstone, and white of egg, and that old-fashioned medicine, Prayer."

The big change, all over Bristol by the 1850's, was the growth of stable populations in the suburbs. The huge growth of population during the Industrial Revolution led to a newly wealthy middle class who wanted to settle in homes of their own. So Clifton stopped being a holiday resort and became a settled suburb—and Redland was born.

As the centre of Bristol became more industrialised, the residents moved outwards. Park Street, as the name implies, was a park, until the 1760's, but otherwise the area up to Cotham and west to the Downs was still farm and commonland. The building boom from the 1840's swallowed it up. Colonel Thomas Tyndall, whose estate was laid out by Humphrey Repton in 1799, as a proper setting for his home, Royal Fort, sold up his 70 acre Tyndall's Park, which was open to the public and stretched as far as Whiteladies Gate, for building plots from 1825 onwards, to some locals' disgust. Samuel

Work-a-day shopping in Hotwell Road around 1900. Little of this scene remains today.

Worrall was doing the same with his land at the top of Blackboy, and Redland Court's 100 acres was sold for building from 1700 onwards, with Redland Manor the last to go, in the 1890's. Between 1820 and 1890, the country became town in west Bristol, and the age of the semi had arrived. (The first semis, on a grand scale, were in fact, Georgian).

The new middle class wanted homes of their own, not homes in a terrace: they wanted a villa, with its association with landed gentry. Those who could not afford a detached villa, bought a semi-detached villa, of the type that can be seen all over Redland, and in and around Pembroke Road. The infilling of farm and parkland was ferocious, and an effect of this passion for villas was a down-grading of the 18th century terrace, which became associated with poverty.

The new home owners (or more commonly, renters) also wanted to live on a hill. Not for the view but for the very practical reason that with no public sewage system, the higher up you lived, the less smelly it was. Hence the popularity of hilly Redland. Up to 1840, the history of Redland was really the history of two estates, Redland Manor and Redland Court. The merchants who owned them got their living from the port trade and from their farms until the American War of Independence and the Napoleonic Wars hit them hard. So unlike Clifton and Hotwells, Redland was, apart from a few Georgian farmhouses and cottages, entirely rural; the transformation in the mid-19th century was dramatic, and very swift. The building schemes were huge: in 1867 one project was to build 300 houses. In fact the haste to erect Redland houses, which were financed by speculators and designed by builders from pattern books, rather than by architects, led to empty rows of unfinished villas which were sold to another speculator to finish, and to collapses. Houses in Clyde Road collapsed overnight because the bow windows were so closely spaced and the party walls so thin, that blasting on a nearby site sent them down like a pack of cards.

The typical Redland villa, with its mock Jacobean or Italian or Greek details was very tasteful in its way, and the houses were very popular, judging from an 1852 advertisement. "To be let: a newly built villa in Redland, with noble dining and drawing rooms, breakfast room, seven bedrooms, two capital and convenient kitchens, two water-closets, soft and spring water, two good cellars, back and front gardens with choice trees, stable for two or three horses, with coach house and sleeping apartment for servant over. The drainage is excellent and the neighbourhood highly respectable, the air is salubrious and the views extensive and picturesque."

The road widths, too, were generous in Redland, and residents fought successfully to save the promenade up to Redland Court (known as Lover's Walk) from development.

Some of the rural character remained: there was still a dairy farm

Fashionable shopping for wealthy Cliftonians: Queens Road and Park Street in their full glory.

in 1878, in fact an outbreak of typhoid in Bristol was traced to milk from this source; other rural qualities were the lack of street lighting and mains drainage, which did not arrive until 1897.

An element which added stability to both Redland and Clifton was the new interest in education. In the 19th century, as now, parents wanted to live in suburbs which had the best schools. Clifton had had, since the late 18th century, a whole rash of private academies, boarding schools and day schools for Young Ladies or Young Gentlemen. They were generally run by genteel and hard-up spinsters, and they offered a minimal education to all but those too poor to pay the fees, right up to the last quarter of the 19th century, when no state education existed and schooling was not compulsory. The 1843 directory lists some 20 of these academies in Clifton, and fairly representative must have been this establishment, advertised in 1851.

It was opened for Young Ladies in Chesterfield Villa, Victoria Park, Clifton by a Mrs Curtis "formerly pupil of Herz, de Corqey and Professor Levi, and many years Governess in the family of the Earl of Aylesford and the Baron de Glaz Malvirade, Paris, whose daughters' education she finished." Mrs Curtis offered the Christian Public a sound religious education, and a useful and accomplished education comprising English, music, singing, French, Italian, German, drawing and painting. She also offered frequent walks and wholesome amusements, a liberal table and kind affectionate treatment. Extras were French conversation with a Parisienne, lectures on philosophical subjects (given by Mrs Curtis) who also gave instruction in arithmetic and the classics. Terms were 30 guineas a term and this school, like all the others, faded out after a few years.

Not all the Clifton establishments for young ladies were quite so salubrious, however. Mrs Walter of 53 Oakfield Road, Clifton offered instruction of a different kind—a chastisement service for girls whose parents were unwilling or unable to thrash their daughters themselves. The service cost £100 a year—slightly more for girls over 20—and was widely advertised in the Bristol papers. A curious editor who sent one of his lady staff to see what Mrs Walter offered found a tall, strong lady, wearing a dress similar to a nurse and a medallion of the Good Shepherd. Her method was to strap girls over a table, with cushions beneath for comfort(!), after stripping down to a dressing gown put on backwards. With "the orthodox surface found at the right angle for punishing," Mrs Walter (or Mrs Walter Smith as she was really named) applied six strokes of the birch on either side, with extra for screams. She also offered a travelling service for parents who didn't wish to call. It was later discovered she was the widow of the former headmaster of All Saints School, Clifton. After his death she ran a school for little

The Paragon in 1962. Clifton before
the onslaught of the motor car.

girls and later (and probably more to her taste) an institute for the education of difficult girls.

But by the 1860's parents wanted something better, for their daughters as well as their sons. The movement for the education of women was strong in Clifton, and it led to the establishment of Clifton High School in 1877. Clifton College, which opened in 1860, impressed parents with its high moral tone (the first headmaster, Dr Percival, made the boys cover their knees when playing football to prevent lascivious thoughts) and by its sensible curriculum, it set higher standards for the other small private schools. Redland, too, began to have a good reputation for its schools, by the 1880's. There was Tudor House, at Cambridge Park, known as Wilkinson's School, after its head. Edward Wilson, who went with Scott to the Antarctic, was a pupil, and wrote: "I never heard a dirty word or doubtful tale or jest there. It was a wonderfully high-toned school." The girls got their high-toned school in 1884 when Redland Court was acquired for Redland High School.

There were of course charity schools and orphanages and reformatories (for the Hopeful Female Discharged Prisoner) and training schools for servants; the Clifton Wood Industrial Training School, at the back of the Mardyke, was opened in 1812 for boys "who otherwise would inevitably have been added to the criminal classes", but not until the Education Act of 1870 was a basic free education available to poor children. In 1870, the Long Room at Hotwells, where the Earl of Jersey in 1743 had entertained 150 to breakfast, became Clifton National School.

By the mid-Victorian period, social life in Hotwells, Clifton and Redland had become neatly stratified. The very rich lived up near the Downs, an expensive area once the Corporation had bought the remaining open land from the Merchant Venturers in 1862, to prevent further building. The middle classes lived in Redland, along Whiteladies Road (known as the Via Sacra because of all the churches) and Pembroke Road, and in Upper Clifton. The less wealthy lived in Lower Clifton, Clifton Wood, while the slopes of Hotwells, and the area down by the water became increasingly a slum area, where servants and dockworkers and poor working class families lived. "An indescribable mass of dingy bricks and mortar, blotched so that the houses look inside out," commented the *Bristol Mercury* in 1884, describing the forlorn contrast between the beauties of the Gorge and the misery of the Hotwells poor.

Each stratum had its entertainments. For the well-off, life revolved mainly around private events, dances, dinners, soirees, concerts. There were visits to the highly respectable Victoria Rooms, opened in 1842, to hear readings by Dickens, song recitals, lectures on aesthetics by Oscar Wilde, and Maskelyne and Cook's Magic Show. The horticultural gardens nearby and the Rifle Drill

Hall next to the University site, had circuses, and the Alexander Hall, in Merchants Road, which seated 500, offered concerts. The Zoo, opened in 1836, was a venue for carnivals and fetes; Blondin performed on the tight-rope in 1861, when 13,000 people flocked to see him sit, kneel and somersault on a rope 70 feet above the ground while blind-folded. Also at the Zoo, the gallant Captain Niblett, captain of the Clifton Cycling Club, led his team in penny-farthing races. The Club also promised assistance to combat the persecution that early cyclists suffered. One of the Club's rules states: "The Club will pay the expenses of any member who prosecutes a person for stone or cap throwing, or other mischievous interference with bicyclists."

Another rather confusing rule read: "A horse shall never be passed on both sides."

The animals seemed to be a minor attraction, and ladies were always writing to the press complaining that they were ill-treated. "Almost all, except the monkeys and the bears, present a forlorn and neglected appearance and several of the wild beasts, notably the hyaena and the puma, have bad wounds which, I am afraid, must be attributed to the keeper," wrote a lady in 1883.

For the poor, there was the Albert Hall, Hotwells, with its variety turns—and pubs. Hotwells was notorious for its pubs, particularly when the temperance movement gripped Bristol in the 1870's, and there was a move for "public houses without the drink." In 1871, between Trinity Church and St Peter's, at the Anchor Road junction, there were 30 pubs within a quarter of a mile. The churches and chapels—there were at least seven in Hotwells by then—provided outings and tea-parties and improving entertainment.

In the second half of the 19th century, the social conscience of the well-off ladies in Clifton and Redland had awoken. Literally hundreds of charitable organisations—often with objectionable titles like The Guild For Poor Things—handed out, if the recipients could stand the patronage, money, food, clothing, blankets, lying-in kits, tickets to see the doctor, and endless advice. The Clifton Dispensary in Dowry Square, opened in 1812, and later the Read Dispensary in Anchor Road, helped with midwifery services and layettes. In the 1870's and onwards, Clifton ladies were agitating about everything: cruelty to animals, votes for women, soup for the needy, temperance for the drunken, training for fallen women and missionaries for Africa.

The suffragettes held regular meetings on the Downs, and the educators, like the Winkworth sisters of Clifton were pressing for places for women at the proposed Bristol University.

Susannah Winkworth's concern was practical: campaigning for better housing for the poor who now mostly lived in the totally

The typical Pembroke Road villa, built during Clifton's Victorian **expansion**.

A once famous Bristol landmark, casualty of road improvements in the 1870s.

The Royal West of England Academy in 1869, as originally built with the grand
entrance at first floor level.

dilapidated Georgian terraces, she tried the experiment of buying several houses in Dowry Square and letting them as flats at low rents. She lived there too, to supervise. The results were so good that she obtained a lease in 1875 to build a model industrial dwelling—virtually Bristol's first apartment block—in Jacob's Wells. For £8,000 she built a "tenement" of 80 flats, each provided with a balcony, water closet and gas. Another large block was put up next door in 1879, and they remained there until the 1950's, grim Scots baronial slums. The 1870's rents were 5s 6d a week for four rooms or 1s 3d for a single room.

But for the most part, the comfortable people of Clifton and Redland led insulated lives. Though Clifton officially became part of Bristol in 1835, in the 1850's a woman was boasting that "she had never been to Bristol". A Mr W P King complained bitterly that he was refused a ticket by the promoter of a subscription ball in Clifton, because he was the son of a tradesman. The area even had its own newspaper, the *Clifton Chronicle* from 1850 to 1928. "Containing besides the ordinary features of a family newspaper, a directory of the inhabitants of Clifton and Redland. As a medium for addressing the upper and middle classes, the Chronicle is unsurpassed."

An insular society bred rows and scandals, the most notable being the Battle of Boyce's Buildings, which raged for a quarter of a century. William Mathias, an eccentric who owned houses in Boyce's buildings, denied carriages, and indeed anything on wheels, including bicycles and perambulators, right of way from the Buildings to Victoria Square. He repeatedly built walls to prevent access and they were knocked down with monotonous regularity. Eventually he put up what is now known as Pharmacy Arch, with an iron gate across it, and this too was frequently removed in the night. The row ended in court in 1861 when Mr Mathias was accused of assaulting a lady who had lifted her perambulator over the gate, no mean feat considering that she was wearing a crinoline! Mathias caught her and pushed her, and the Corporation brought the action. The case was discharged and when they tried to bring another, there was a huge petition in Clifton on Mathias's behalf. He became known locally as The General because of his obsession about rights of way, a permanent topic of discussion when so many roads were privately owned.

Another Clifton character was the builder-architect J W King, whose projects always seemed to fail. In 1873, he tried to bring fashionable shopping to Whiteladies Road by building a grand Royal Arcade (between West Park and Aberdeen Road). Another unrealised scheme was to bridge Perry Road to Small Street with a viaduct. His most potent ambition was to have a street named after him, and in 1879 he achieved it, when he opened his Royal Bazaar

Fairs were held at Bristol Zoo in Victorian times.

and Winter Garden off Boyce's Avenue, in King's Road. The bazaar, built on two floors, with arcades, still stands, tantalisingly private, the property of Knee Bros., who took it over a few years later, when the project failed. Where the modern shops stand in front of it was his 20,000 square foot Winter Garden. It cost King in all £10,000; how gratified he would be to see that the street still bears his name.

Another commercial shopping project that was only a partial success in Clifton Village was the department store of J Cordeux and Sons. F Cordeux, another branch of the family, had been trading in St James Barton since the 1840's; in the 1870's, the firm opened up on the corner of Merchants Road and Regent Street, selling drapery, hats, haberdashery, toys, underclothes and furnishings, all Wonderfully Cheap. In its heyday, the store occupied all the houses on the site of the present car showroom, and stretched round to the Post Office, while the auction rooms were their warehouse.

Upstairs was a tea-room and a huge workroom where 400 staff made up clothes to order: some of the staff lived in, in Saville Place. But snooty Clifton cannot have provided enough custom, for the firm moved out in 1909 to what was a far more successful shopping centre for Clifton, the elegant Royal Parade or Promenade in Queens Road, built in 1859. (The upper facade is mainly unaltered to this day.)

This was the first purpose-built parade of shops in the area and it attracted up-market retailers and a big and fashionable Clifton clientele.

Meanwhile, in Hotwells, there was a burst of prosperity. The Hotwell Road was widened in 1849, and had gradually been built up with a flourishing row of shops, running without a break from Anchor Road to Dowry Square, on both sides of the road. There were, in 1883, 53 different trades being carried out there, and unbelievably, to those who live in the almost shopless area now, there were besides the inevitable 23 pubs, ten butchers, three fishmongers, 12 greengrocers, seven refreshment rooms, ten bakers, five tailors, six tobacconists, two hairdressers, three drapers, six grocers and two chemists. This profusion of shops continued right up to the First World War, and Hotwells even had a cinema from the silent film days until 1939.

Clifton, too, went through a bad patch; even in the 1890's, the big villas were being divided up into flats, and as the supply of servants slowed down, following the 1870 Education Act, the terraces increasingly became the homes of poorer families, except for the area near the Suspension Bridge. The Depression, and then the Second World War, meant continued neglect, and it was not until the affluent 1960's that the professional classes began to move back and restore the now distinctly shabby terraces.

Redland, too, became bedsitter land, with the grand villas divided up into flats and single rooms, as owners or landlords without batteries of cheap servants, struggled to bring enough income to keep the houses in repair.

In the 1890's, there were great worries about the large number of houses left empty and unlet, just as there had been a century before, the quandary being that if rents were lowered, the "wrong" sort of people would move into the area. Clifton and Redland hung on desperately to their gentility, and the flavour of the period before World War One is superbly captured in the novels of E H Young.

Emily Hilda Young married Bristol solicitor J A H Daniell in 1902, and they lived in Clifton until 1917, when he was killed at Ypres. Besides causing a scandal by going to live with a married headmaster in a ménage à trois, E H Young wrote nine novels, six of which are set in Clifton and Hotwells. She sardonically observed the genteel church-dominated lives of the ladies who lived near Christchurch Green, and the sad and shabby lives of the shop-keepers and servants who lived on the slopes of Hotwells, describing the area so accurately that you can actually pinpoint each house which she uses as a setting. She was aware, too, of the sense of the past that still pervades Clifton.

"It was the houses that gave its character to the street, and here, as elsewhere, the gently persistent personality of the place remained unmoved by any material or spiritual changes since the first red bricks were well and truly laid. It was like a masterpiece of portrait painting in which a person of another generation looks down on his descendants and dominates them. Even where the old houses had disappeared, their ghosts seemed to hover over the streets."

The pattern of boom and bust in Clifton and Hotwells was continued well into this century, according to the pensioners who remember the area from the turn of the century. An 84 year old man who was born in The Mall, said: "Clifton when I was a boy was a very genteel place: most of the big houses were privately owned by people who had servants, and the shops in the village were all top quality. There were carnivals at the Zoo, and I can remember the excitement amongst us boys as we saw the first motor cars up on Christchurch Green, where the richest people lived. Clifton was very quiet, very respectable.

"But that changed in the Second World War. All those big houses were sold off for ludicrous prices—just a few hundred pounds—because there were no more servants to keep them going. The servants went to do war work. So the houses in Royal York Crescent and The Mall and Caledonia Place were all divided into cheap flats at very low rents. There were no grants during the war to do them up, so the places got more and more shabby, and it remained like that until the sixties. Clifton was the place where

The Arch at Boyces Avenue, Clifton. Little changed since this photograph was taken in the early 1960s.

students came for cheap lodgings. The terraces came up again after the sixties but a lot of them are still flats. Expensive flats instead of cheap ones!

"The place looks very much the same, though, apart from a few new buildings, but the style of the shops has changed completely. I remember how the shop-keepers would all deliver—they kept horses and carts—but now it's all antique shops and restaurants."

Of Hotwells, he remembered: "It was definitely a working class district, most of the people who lived there worked on the Docks. I wouldn't call it a slum, but there were bad housing conditions: the old houses had no water and outside lavatories and they were damp and neglected. Hotwells was famous for its pubs: there seemed to be one every ten yards. They were open all day when I was a boy, and the seamen who came into the Docks drank there. They liked their beer—it was 1d a pint! Before the First World War and up to the Second, the Hotwell Road was a busy shopping street, but I can recall that it was going down, even in the thirties. When the trams finished, the Hotwell Road was widened, and all the little courts and alleys and squares that were on the Clifton Wood side were demolished.

"The people that lived there were rehoused out of the area, and so there weren't enough customers to keep the shops going, especially during the Depression. The area is still a disgrace: the Corporation should have planned a redevelopment along there years ago. The state of the Hotwell Road put a blight on the area, and it's only recently that things have begun to improve, with the building of new flats. Where Rownham Mead stands now was a cattle market: the Irish boats used to bring cattle in, and as boys, we'd go down and watch them being slaughtered."

The speaker is one of the few Bristolians still living who can boast that he drank the Hot Well water. "As a boy, I used to go cycling along the towpath that is now the Portway, and on the way there was a drinking fountain served by the Hotwell spring. I drank that water regularly, though I can't recall what it tasted like."

Another 83 year old lady who lived near the Rocks Railway as a child says that its closure in 1934 came as a blow. "All the Hotwells folk used it like a bus to get up to Clifton to the shops. We resented having to walk up the zig-zag of Granby Hill! It was 1½d up and 1d down and we used to shout in the tunnel to make echoes. The river must have been a lot cleaner then, because I remember that a shopkeeper near the bottom of Freeland Place used to go catching shrimps at Pill. He sold them for 4d a pint, and we all complained when he put the price up to 6d. Occasionally he'd have salmon for sale too, caught further up the Avon. Unbelievable!

"We played a lot around the waterfront, fishing in the river: the boys swam there, but we didn't dare. We used to wave to the

32

steamers coming through the Gorge and throw things at them from the Suspension Bridge.

"Hotwells was a very working class district, but friendly, and we had wonderful shops. The population was much greater then, with all the little houses that have been demolished to make way for the Cumberland Basin flyover, and the hundreds of poor houses on the Clifton Wood slopes. The Hotwell Road used to be packed with people shopping and going to the pubs. We even had a cinema!

"During the Second World War, if you lived in one of the Georgian houses, you were thought lucky, because they had basements and cellars to shelter in. Those who didn't used to shelter in the railway tunnel just beyond the Colonnade: you had to start queuing at 3pm in the afternoon to get a place for the night. Later on in the war it was closed, because the Corporation stored the city treasures there.

"Clifton before the Second World War was a lovely place: so quiet. The shops closed on Saturday afternoons, until Woolworths came and stayed open all Saturday. The others had to follow suit."

Some of the Hotwells women worked as cleaners in the big Clifton houses. An 82 year old woman who lived in the Hotwell Road from 1911 onwards was a general servant to various families in Sion Hill and The Mall. "It was hard work, all those grates to clean and stairs to climb with buckets of coal. I didn't live in, but quite a few of the servants did, they had rooms in the basements. I used to earn about 6d an hour. Clifton wasn't exactly posh, but it was comfortable. Most families would employ a general servant and a cleaner, and the richest had cooks and nannies as well. One of the families I worked for was the Livermores, who owned the People's Palace Cinema in Baldwin Street: Mr Livermore was very generous, he used to arrange outings for the old folk. But the tone of Clifton went down during the second war, the prosperous families left, and the houses were all turned into cheap flats.

"In Hotwells, there were lots of poor families, living in flats in the big Georgian houses. All Dowry Square was flats, and in Lebeck House, where Garrick House flats are, there were dozens of families. Some of them were squatters. Lots of the little cottages had no water, they had to use a pump in the street. It was no wonder we had all those pubs—you needed somewhere to go to get away from home. There were lots of chapels and missions too: I can remember at least seven, and there was a Salvation Army and a Seamen's Mission too. We got very annoyed when the lady who ran the fish and chip shop in Chapel Row got religion and became a missionary, and closed the shop!

"Before the Hillsborough flats were built in the Hotwell Road, there was a row of cottages there, with alleys and courts behind, all dreadful slums. The Prince of Wales came to open these new flats in

1935. There was a huge fuss, bands, processions, and I believe the Prince said in his speech that the Hillsborough flats were the best flats in the West of England. And look at them now!

"I don't live in the past, I don't believe in it, but I do think that Hotwells and Clifton were nicer places to live in the 1920's. I'm glad to see Hotwells is coming up again. We've waited long enough."

Gateway to the World

James Belsey enthuses over the suburbs around The Downs.

This is ancient land and you can still see the signs in eroded hill forts and creeks which were once harbours; in lost estates, and the lines of roads which the Romans once knew. It is a land of soft hills and downs, set against dramatic cliffs, great rivers, woods and silvery streams. It is a countryside which has been, by turns, wilderness and then stronghold, pleasure grounds for landed gentry, farmland and pasture, dreamscapes for poets and painters and, above all, a place to escape from city life to find fresh air and freedom.

The Avon Gorge has been one of England's most important gateways to the world and has witnessed the departure of scores of generations of adventurers, merchants, warriors and explorers along the Avon and from the ports of Sea Mills, Bristol and Avonmouth.

Only in the last century or so has Bristol crept up the hillsides and across the fields, spreading its tendrils along improved roads, tramway lines, bus routes and, finally, today's car-choked commuter runs.

We call it North West Bristol but this part of old Gloucestershire is centuries older than the city that used to lie below it and now envelops it. The Romans knew Sea Mills and Shirehampton long before the acres around the confluence of the Rivers Frome and Avon were settled, fortified and later developed into a town. North West Bristol is defined in this book as a rough triangle with the Downs as the base. Two sides of the triangle are natural—the Avon Gorge, that gigantic, spectacular ha-ha which brings city and wild country closer together in Bristol than in any other city I know, and the huge sweep of the Severn estuary. The third side is arbitrary and follows a line that heads in a northerly direction from Coldharbour Road and Kellaway Avenue up through Southmead.

This wide area includes suburbs like Westbury Park, Stoke Bishop and Sneyd Park clustering around the Downs, Westbury-on-Trym in the valley below, and, beyond that, the hilly, still wooded communities of Shirehampton, Henbury, Brentry and Coombe Dingle with Sea Mills (the Roman port of Abonae) in the shelter of the great curves of the Avon in its final miles before joining the open waters of the Bristol Channel.

The Downs is one of the loveliest city areas remaining in Europe and its survival as open land has dictated the pattern of suburban development in North West Bristol. It acts as a perfect buffer zone between inner Bristol, and the communities which have sprung up alongside and beyond its acres of rolling grassland. It has long been a huge attraction to people from all parts of Bristol. When there was something to celebrate, this was one of the most important places to gather. In 1822 the *Bristol Journal* recorded a May Day programme on Durdham Down which offered such varied delights as horse racing, "sporting the light fantastic toe", fisticuffs in which Jacky Cabbage "shewed to challenge Hazell for a bellyful", (of beer, one supposes,) and a dinner and ball to round off the whole affair at sundown.

These were the times when the chimney sweeps would come up from the city wearing brightly coloured streamers, collecting money from onlookers who watched them dance. In the early 19th century the Downs were still open country and it didn't matter too much if the revels got a little out of hand and you had to pick your way among the stupified and dead drunk. But as the area became more gentrified, so the rowdy races and celebrations began to be frowned upon and they disappeared, one by one.

You can still find the odd survivor, though, even today. Regular fun fairs are still held at holiday times on the Downs and the area really comes to life each summer when the Bristol Flower Show brings thousands from across the West Country.

It was in May 1861 that the Downs, the 230 acres of Clifton Down and the 211 acres of Durdham Down, came into corporate ownership, ensuring that the public would continue to have free access to this land. A correspondent to the *Bristol Mirror* wrote in celebration at the news: "The beautiful scenery of the Avon, the pure fresh air from the distant sea, know no caste. They are free to be enjoyed by the most lowly. The poor man may watch the white-winged craft come up the winding Avon; he may see the sun descending in all its gorgeous magnificence—he may contemplate the thousand tints of Leigh Woods".

The Clifton and Durdham Down Act of 1861 ensured suburban development. Victorian Bristol was a rapidly expanding city and the better-off wanted to escape the muck and grime of the congested central areas. The now secure, open Downs were an obvious magnet to developers who saw golden opportunities to build streets and estates around the park.

The Downs are less spectacular than they were. Sheep grazing ended with the Second World War and the brilliantly coloured, flower-studded acres have muted into a uniform green, thanks to mechanical mowing. The prevailing south westerly winds still carry seed up from the wilderness of the Avon Gorge, but you have to search hard to find the rarer wild flowers. The spectacular views so often painted, have been limited in many directions, because the sheep once kept the scrub at grazing level. Now the cliff edges are a jungle of tall bushes and dense undergrowth. It is only when poor weather makes grass-cutting impossible for several weeks on end in

The Downs in quieter days. Sheep grazed here until the
Second World War.

38

early or midsummer that you can get some idea of what the Downs must have looked like to the first North West Bristol suburbanites a century or so ago. Look closely in the spring and you can still find a few remaining colonies of cowslips which once grew in such profusion that children made chains and necklaces of them. Then comes the really brilliant flowering, with dazzling waves of buttercups, the soft yellows of little black medic and the richer oranges of the vetches with, here and there, the delicate blues of the harebells that still survive. I wish at least one true meadow on the Downs could be left so that the wild flowers, for which it was once so famous, could grow again.

Westbury Park has the broadest, finest prospect of all the Downs suburbs. Stand with your back to the handsome Victorian villas on Westbury Park itself in winter when the trees are bare and all you can see is grassland, wild woods and the tower of Abbots Leigh parish church, with just a glimpse of Sneyd Park to remind you that you're still in a great city. It was just the spot for wealthy Victorians who wanted imposing positions for new houses beyond the growing sprawl of Redland and well away from the crowds and filth of the city.

By the 1830's, the area had already been brought into Bristol as the city's boundaries extended. In the 1860's, building began in earnest with the attractive Cambridge Park development with its lion-topped pillars and villas in adjoining Westbury Park. Until then, this had been farming country and you can still see traces of its past in the little cottages by the Cambridge Inn on Coldharbour Road. They recall the days when this was Cold Harbour Lane leading to Cold Harbour farm.

Rich families with horse-and-carriage transport took advantage of the improving roads and became daily commuters. They were the new rich—lawyers and bank managers, industrialists and entre-preneurs. They called their neighbourhood Westbury Park because it was the parkland above the village of Westbury.

By the 1880's the suburb had developed into a busy place with little streets behind the grander homes with their frontages on the Downs. In Berkley, Victoria, Albert and Etloe roads were the terraced houses of the families who provided the labour and services to the rich folk who lived in the smart mansions.

Once the horse-drawn buses and, later, the trams had arrived, the area mushroomed. Speculative builders threw up networks of Edwardian terraces and, after the First World War, when all building ground to a halt, the in-filling process continued, spreading into Henleaze as land ran out.

The heyday of the grander houses is over. They have either been converted into smaller units or found new uses, like the Westbury Park villas which now form St Christopher's School. But the smaller streets have become some of Bristol's more sought-after homes. It's interesting to recall that this now largely middle-class area was once considered a hotbed of socialism. The Red Menace, according to the recollections of Mr Bert Spiller, in the delightful pamphlet *Westbury Park Not So Long Ago*, was to be found in Victoria Road, of all places. He remembered an early Bristol socialist called Sweetman who preached a heady brand of left-wing politics. But it obviously wasn't all radicalism here because Victoria Road was also the home of the young Jack Board, the great Gloucestershire wicket keeper who learnt his skill bouncing balls off the lamp-posts of Westbury Park. The children referred to the different areas on the east side of the Downs as the patches—"See you on the second patch, then".

They would cross the bumpy, half mile or so in summer and look at the mansions of Sneyd Park which lay on the other side of Durdham Down. Walk over today and you'll risk your neck trying to dash between the busy traffic on the main roads.

Sneyd Park was one of the West Country's smartest suburbs right from the start, and for good reason. It has all the grandeur and roomy feel of high Victorian and Edwardian architecture and planning. Garden lovers can't fail to be impressed by the now mature trees planted as Sneyd Park was built—great cedars of Lebanon, lofty redwoods, gaunt Scots pine and spectacular blue cedars.

This was once a country estate, Old Sneed Park, owned by the Jackson family, but by the 1850's the Jacksons' descendants saw far more of a future turning the acres into a suburb of houses than by trying to make a living off the land. In 1853, James Martin, a Jackson descendant and principal owner in the area, began his successful attempt to build a new Sneyd park. Martin pointed out that market forces were all in favour of houses, not fields, on his land. As he said: "Many dwelling houses have been and are being built in the district nearto and there is a great and increasing demand in the district for building leases for long terms of years and the devised estates comprise many eligible situations for the erection of detached villas and other houses and are otherwise from their proximity to the city of Bristol and to Clifton very conveniently situated for building purposes." He was right, of course, and the planners agreed. And so sprang up that marvellous frontage of great semi-detached mansions along Rockleaze, four storeys tall, faced with stone and decorated with great bays. Development of the acres beyond the Downs quickly followed with a continuing emphasis on large, luxurious homes. Sneyd Park quickly established its reputation as Bristol's richest, smartest suburb, easily surpassing the older, more crowded terraces, squares and crescents of Clifton.

Westbury-on-Trym and Kellaway Avenue.

But there were some initial difficulties, not least of them communications with Bristol, where most of the new Sneyd Parkers worked. It is ironic that a Roman road crosses the Downs and passes through Sneyd Park on its way to Sea Mills while the Victorian residents had no direct route. They either took a bumpy carriage ride across the wheel-rutted route to Blackboy Hill or they followed the circuitous route along the winding road that took pleasure seekers from Clifton to the Sea Walls.

It was only when the suburb became a part of Bristol at last that the city's leaders allowed today's throughfare to be cut across from Blackboy Hill.

Sneyd Park's sense of exclusivity hasn't been lost. It has often been nick-named "Snide Park" and some say it's a snooty sort of place. It certainly has a quiet sense of dignity, respectability and cosy grandeur. That mood has not been lost by the large-scale redevelopments which have taken place since the Second World War. Some of the early mansions have been demolished to be replaced by bland and inoffensive, low-rise but decidedly up-market blocks of flats often hidden by the mature trees planted by Victorians. Other large 19th century houses have been gutted and redesigned internally, their scale perfect for conversion into expensive flats.

Diehards complain that Sneyd Park has lost its rural quality and yearn for the days when the lanes were a bit wilder and woolier, the stone walls unbroken by constant interruptions for gateways for new flats and houses and the population rather smaller than it is today. But, because of the nature of the area, its wooded appearance, its contours, the high quality of the buildings and mature, screened gardens, it never seems anything but a backwater, well out of the reach of the city.

Sneyd Park and Stoke Bishop merge into each other gracefully. Stoke Bishop is middle-class suburbia too, not as dramatic as its neighbour and rather showier in some ways. The Victorians planted great trees—Stoke Bishop planted flowering cherries.

There are some nice anecdotes, particularly, in the place names of Stoke Bishop. Pitch and Pay Lane, for instance, the spot where, it was said, farmers used to pitch their products across to the people of Bristol when the city was suffering from one of its many outbreaks of plague. Pay? The Bristolians threw back money in exchange and the farmers walked off happy with a deal that avoided direct contact with the suspect townspeople. Parry's Lane is another. Supposedly a corruption of Paddy's Well Lane, a quiet country lane with a pump where horses could be watered. The pump was always known as Paddy's Well. Paddy's Well, Parry's . . . names can change very quickly in an area which turns from country to city.

Stoke Bishop was growing when Mr 'Tony' Stirret first knew it.

Interior — White Horse Inn, Westbury-on-Trym in 1957.

He watched it develop into a thriving suburb, just as he saw the accompanying rise of Henleaze and the continuing prosperity of Sneyd Park and Westbury Park. Mr Stirret runs the butcher's shop his father built in North View, Westbury Park, more than half a century ago. His is a typical story of a Bristol family which made the move to the new opportunities and surroundings of North West Bristol. He recalled: "We were living in St George before we came up here. My father had a butcher's shop at 137 Church Road, Redfield and it was a good shop. But father wanted to get on in the world and he'd a real hankering to move up to the north west side of Bristol, like so many people.

"It was a good area to come to—still is, it hasn't changed much that way. When I was a small lad, say nine or ten, we would come up on Sunday on the bus, in the days when you could sit in front with the driver, and we'd get off at Westbury Park.

"Then father would walk us around the district and look for the place we were going to live one day. He took a special liking to the house on the corner of Howard Road and Linden Road, the house that used to be the dentist's place, but it wasn't on the market. Instead he discovered that there was building land available where they were going to extend one side of North View and he began building this shop in 1927 and he opened the following year. I soon got to know all this part of Bristol, Stoke Bishop, Sneyd Park, Westbury Park, Henleaze and the nearer bits of Redland. It was bicycle delivery in those days, mind you!

"I was started in the business as a boy. Even when we were in Redfield father used to get me to work. When I was at Bristol Grammar School, father used to make out a sort of sick note so that I could work for the shop on a Saturday. Northumbria Drive wasn't cut in those days and we looked out over open country. It was a country estate and Westbury Cricket Club had their grounds up here then. Henleaze was a pretty small place and Westbury Park consisted of grand houses and then the small streets where the less well-off lived. I suppose they were people like clerks, that sort of person.

"Stoke Bishop and Sneyd Park seemed much the same although, of course, there are many more houses but they're still very well-to-do, just as they've always been. It was exciting watching these suburbs growing. I can remember the fun when the Orpheus Cinema was being built—and I can remember it closing down when they turned the site into Waitrose.

"Our business prospered with all the development around us and there was one great day for us, in 1933, when father won third prize at Smithfield for his pork sausages—the third best in the whole of the country! I've still got the certificate in the shop. He kept the recipe in his head—he would never write it down. At one time we

Henleaze Road shops in the 1960s.

had nine of us working in this little shop in North View. It seems incredible today, in the 1980's, but that's how the shops round here were run. There was father, the three married men he employed, two or three delivery boys with the bicycles parked outside the front, a girl in the office and me. You wouldn't find that nowadays.''

Much, much older than the suburbs that have grown up around the Downs is the village of Westbury on the river Trym, once a far wider, deeper waterway than today. It's hard to imagine Vikings sailing up the river to sack the Saxon village of Westbury or 'Wesbyrig'—but they did. The church was destroyed by these unwelcome visitors but it was rebuilt again and again over the centuries and Westbury and its near neighbour, Henbury, were well-established communities long before Bristol engulfed them.

Westbury's greatest asset is that it still, despite all the development, retains a truly village atmosphere. When people talk of "Westbury village", the phrase means something in this part of Bristol. The High Street may have been changed in part by a proliferation of banks and building societies, but it is still clearly a village high street, with a definite centre around the war memorial.

Twenty years ago, when Westbury was celebrating the 1,250th anniversary of the church's Saxon foundation, Mr E H Mogford, who had taken a life-long interest in local history, put down his memories for future generations.

He remembered a time when Westbury was a group of houses and farms built around a village green which was known as The Batch. A huge elm tree once stood near the site of today's Post Office and there was a pound for stray animals and some village stocks where miscreants could be fettered. Waters Lane was known at the turn of the century as Betty Waters Lane after an old woman who lived in a cottage there and sold well water of such reputed medicinal quality that people travelled for miles for some of her magical Adam's Ale. The village blacksmith was only a step or two away.

But Westbury's story is far grander than that of a pleasant little village built around a river. A Benedictine monastery was founded here in the 11th century and at the end of the 12th century it had become a collegiate church. Its fame grew and its ecclesiastical stars included that great man of the Reformation, Dean John Wycliffe.

The area's prestige attracted wealthy commuters from Bristol centuries before today's housing estates sprang up. The imposing St Monica's Home of Rest is built on the site of Cote House, home of the rich brothers Thomas and Josiah Wedgewood and a place of welcome for poets and writers. Visitors included the poets Coleridge, Wordsworth and Southey. There is still a Southey House in Westbury Hill, although it isn't certain if this was the house where the Poet Laureate lived during his stay in Westbury, a spell

Sylvan Coombe Dingle and a quiet High Street, Shirehampton.

August Bank Holiday at Blaise, 1955.

in which he "never before or since produced so much poetry in the same space of time".

Another famous short-term resident was the late Indira Gandhi, a contemporary of the writer Iris Murdoch, at Badminton School. Mrs Gandhi, by then Prime Minister of India, had fond memories of Westbury from her school days.

"My memories of the parish of Westbury are pleasant and interesting," she recalled. "My sojourn at Badminton School was an experience which was a valuable one and which played a part in widening the horizons of my mind and in shaping my personality. I remember, too, the long walks and the fascinating stories of old Bristol."

One story she must have heard concerned a tomb in the parish church graveyard. The inscription reads: "To the memory of Richard Ruddle, Sir Robert Cann's Coachman, robbed and murdered by Burnett and Payne, October 27, 1743, aged 52 years". The murder had taken place on the Downs, and Burnett and Payne, the last highwaymen to menace the area, were captured and hanged.

Westbury-on-Trym has grown in an orderly sort of way. Its near neighbour, Henbury, can't be said to have done the same. The heart of Henbury around the old ford and by the parish church could be in the middle of the country—if you can close your eyes to the garish Salutation pub or the insensitive council estates (the first of which went up in the 1950's) on the hillside. Bristol didn't take over Henbury until 1935 and it hasn't done much to improve it.

Vine House in Henbury Road, once the home of the Pountney family who founded Bristol Pottery, has a remarkable garden, created from rough land by Professor Tom Hewer and his wife Ann, who moved there just after the Second World War. They used sticks and strings and gangs of students to mark out the planting area of what has become one of the finest private gardens in the region. Its shrubs are now mature and the collection of plants is fascinating. The garden is open to the public on occasional weekends.

Henbury's history is largely built around Henbury Manor. The late 17th century mansion once commanded the surrounding lands, rubbing shoulders with other handsome estates such as King's Weston and Blaise. In the churchyard of St Mary in Henbury there is the obelisk to Sir Robert Southwell of King's Weston and, most touching of all, the gravestone of the negro servant of the Earl of Suffolk, one Scipio Africanus. The inscription reads: "I who was born a Pagan and a Slave now sweetly sleep a Christian in my grave".

Blaise, around the corner, has one of the most interesting housing developments in Britain, the charming Blaise Hamlet. Designed by John Nash, architect of London's Regent street, in 1809 and completed within two years, it was built to house pensioners from

John Harford's neighbouring Blaise estate in a romantic, rustic setting—a prototype garden city development. Nash incorporated all the features he thought the perfect mini-suburb should have—individual buildings, a green, a sundial and a parternalistic sense of community.

But Blaise Hamlet, pretty though it is, wasn't always quite so cosy. Mrs Marjorie Hellen, for many years the postmistress at Blaise, and who was born at Oak Cottage in the Hamlet in 1901, told me: "There were three of us children all in one bed until my brother grew too big and he had to move out to sleep above the post office, which had been in our family since mid-Victorian times. It was cold in winter unless you were by the range and in the summer the green was a meadow and they could come in high summer and cut the hay with scythes. All our water was from the pump across on the green and as children we'd play in the fields and trees—all the fields had ponds in those days and children were often falling in. There were lots of children in the hamlet then. We would see lots of painters in the summer, because Blaise Hamlet was always a popular subject for artists".

It's strange to think that the scheme pioneered by Nash played a part in the development of the garden city movement and that the thinking that lay behind the creation of the between-the-wars council housing of North West Bristol was inspired by Nash and Blaise. The estates were created as part of the great drive to rehouse the poorer citizens of Bristol well away from the appalling conditions of the inner city. Despite this well-intentioned resettling, the communities, dislocated from their cheek-by-jowl existence in central Bristol, lost heart.

The saga of rehousing folk from the city slums to new suburbs has been related in other sections of this book. The experiences of those who moved to Southmead exactly mirror those of Filwood Park and other estates south of the Avon. The same initial sense of freedom and relief, the same delight in a well-built, tidy house then the gradual disillusionment, sense of isolation and wearisome distance from work in the city and heavy burden of travelling costs on limited family budgets. The process continued after the Second World War with fresh efforts to rehabilitate the thousands of families living in sub-standard homes, leading to new estates at Lawrence Weston as well as extending Shirehampton, Southmead and other pre-war developments. It's all too easy with the benefit of hindsight to point out all the failures of the suburban council estates, but it should be remembered that they were built by well-meaning civic leaders who were convinced that the priority was to build as many homes as cheaply and quickly as possible for families who desperately needed somewhere decent to live.

And, after all, North West Bristol has provided homes in an area which has long been one of the most sought-after places to live in the region. King's Weston House, Vanburgh's great masterpiece, overlooks Lawrence Weston and Shirehampton. The whole of this corner of today's city is scattered with the homes of the rich and famous from the past, all attracted by its position and the countryside.

Shirehampton has a Roman villa and up at Blaise there is a pre-Roman hillfort, showing that man has found this little bit of England a good place to settle since before recorded history began. Its wooded hills and valleys, its dramatic rivers and cliffs, its Downs and, above all, its often stunning sense of open-ness and space in a great provincial city, make North West Bristol remarkable.

Ethel Thomas, that excellent historian of the Avonmouth/ Shirehampton area, is right to rebuke those who fail to revel in the area's great assets. What she writes in *Shirehampton Story* is true of much of the rest of North West Bristol.

"Whether or not modern man-made features have helped enhance Shirehampton views or not is a matter of personal choice, but what is so regrettable is that Shirehampton no longer takes a great pride in her God-given panoramic views, as was the case in the 18th and 19th centuries when they were considered a main tourist attraction.

"Neither does Shirehampton sing their praises—and alas the magnificent views these days are either taken for granted or ignored altogether!"

Atmospheric Somerset Street, Kingsdown in the 1960s.

The Hangman Hanged and the Curate Frustrated

David Harrison looks at the communities which spread on both sides of the road to the north.

The traveller heading out of Bristol to the north follows the age-old road towards Gloucester through areas which sum up, more than any others, the growth of the suburbs of Bristol.

From the historic city centre, the road turns into Stokes Croft, now a slightly seedy area but once lined with trees and a favourite walk for Bristolians.

On the left is Kingsdown, originally the place where the king's horses were exercised and another popular leisure area before the developers moved in. To the right, Montpelier and Ashley, rolling downs once covered by fields and orchards, and St Pauls with its graceful town houses lining City Road. A little further, past John Foster's attractive Arley Chapel, is Cotham, an area which would have been developed at the same time as Kingsdown, had the money not run out.

Pass beneath the great railway arches, built in 1874 at the height of the great railway boom, and you are in Victorian and Edwardian Bristol. Redland stretches up to the left, then Bishopston, a newer district created only in the 1850's, while to the right is St Andrews, a solid, prosperous area set around a graceful park.

Beyond the evidence of Victorian expansion is ancient Horfield, once a separate village with its own Lord of Manor but now a rather dull, anonymous place.

With the exception of Kingsdown, and part of Cotham which was close enough to the city to attract some of the earliest suburbs, virtually all the development of this area started in the second half of the last century.

Bristol was an appalling place in Victorian times. A survey in 1845 after a cholera outbreak which killed three per cent of the population (a figure exceeded by only two other places in England) showed many parts of Bristol and Clifton were totally without sewerage. Those that did have drains sent the effluent straight into the stagnant harbour, and the Frome through the city was little more than an open sewer. "The stench which spread from it every summer sufficed to turn weak stomachs", wrote John Latimer less than half a century later.

No wonder those who could afford it wanted to get out, although they didn't do much better in Redland, Cotham or Kingsdown where conditions were almost as bad well into the 1860's.

What the middle classes wanted were decent houses outside the city walls but not so far that they couldn't travel into the city to work. The railways, the horse buses and finally the trams all helped put pressure on the open countryside to the north of Bristol by making access easier. The commuter age had arrived.

It is worth going back to look at Bristol in 1830, the year that the first Ordnance Survey one inch to a mile map was published. The map shows Kingsdown already established but the city stops at Stokes Croft. There is no St Pauls but Baptist Mills was there and houses are already spreading across the hills of Montpelier. Ashley Court was still standing, a mansion flattened between 1872-6 together with a farmhouse in which Cromwell is supposed to have slept before the second seige of Bristol. Both were replaced by new houses for which, contemporary reports record, there was a very great demand. It was hardly surprising for even today it is easy to imagine the glorious views across the city to Kelston Tump above Bath and the Dundry hills.

To the left of the Gloucester Road, the map shows Redland Court and Redland Lodge, and a short road leading to a farm called Cold Harbour, now remembered in Coldharbour Road.

Further north there are scattered cottages but little before Horfield which stood where Kellaway Avenue now joins the main Gloucester Road on what remains of the common. After that, open countryside past Southmead wood to the sizeable village of Filton.

By 1887 when photographs of the city were taken from a balloon the picture is very different. Clifton has expanded considerably and now merges with Kingsdown, Cotham and Redland—rows of neatly laid out houses stretching across the north west edge of the city. Stokes Croft is heavily built up and what we now call St Pauls links Kingsdown with sprawling east Bristol. Further out, Montpelier is still fairly rural but the lower roads of St Andrews already run parallel to the Gloucester Road and Berkeley Road and Egerton Road are established at the centre of the new suburb of Bishopston. Part of Somerville Road has been built, leading up to those houses on Ashley Hill and their wonderful views across rolling hills and fields.

In east and south Bristol, however, the prospect is very different—hundreds of tall factory chimneys, a surprising number of glass kilns and rows of terraced houses. No wonder the better-off headed towards the comparatively rural settlements to the west and north. By this time, Kingsdown was already 150 years old. The attractive slopes were originally owned by the Montague family and were bought in 1737 by one Giles Greville, a wealthy apothecary. He saw the potential as a building site and laid out the land but got little further than putting up an inn, the noted Montague Tavern. For some reason, development was slow. Two houses were built in Southwell Street in 1740 and one called Wints Folly, complete with

Cheltenham Road floods in the 1920s.

gazebo on the roof, was advertised in 1750, but it took until the 1780's for the area to be really built up.

It was not without opposition. One Bristolian wrote to *Felix Farley's Journal* in 1760 complaining that the public was about to be deprived of one of the pleasantest walks in the area. "Kingsdown, delightful spot, is already beginning to be dug up and to experience the rude, deforming labours of the delving masons," he complained rather poetically.

Another writer was even more acid. He sent in a poem to the *Journal* the following year, castigating the tradesmen who felt they were going up in the world by living above the city:

> "Each petty tradesman here must have a seat
> And vainly thinks the height will make him great
> But little things look less the more they rise
> So wrens may mount until they look like flies.
> Haste brewer e'er too late and choose thy spot
> Sell of thy soot and build thy Kingsdown cot
> Come hither pedlars, quit your dusty stalls
> Here build your seats, on rise your garden walls
> And when you've built it o'er call it what you will
> 'Twill not be Kingsdown then but Pedlars Hill."

Such scorn had little effect and the development of Kingsdown continued. It is easy to understand why some Bristolians felt so bitter about it because those in the old walled city would send their children up on the down for a change of air in the summer.

King Square, at the bottom of the hill, was laid out in 1755 and named New Square. It was designed by George Tully who also laid out Dowry Square and Brunswick Square, and he himself lived in a house there. There were several schools for young gentlemen and Miss Pike's school for young ladies, while at No 18 was Mr Ash who made his fortune from a sweet factory, raisin wine and raspberry brandy.

One house in the square was advertised in 1762 as offering "two large arched cellars, two handsome parlours and a large dining room, all neatly wainscotted and ornamented with enriched cornishes (sic), two curious marble chimney pieces with pattern tile and entrance panelled, with stout, good lodging rooms, two large garretts, several closets and good pantries, two large kitchens, both sorts of water, oven, clamp kiln, stewholes and other conveniences, large, three stall stable and coach house with lofts over and a handsome garden." It shows the type of resident Tully had in mind.

But living at the bottom of the hill had distinct disadvantages. Sewage from Montague Parade (now Kingsdown Parade) ran down an open gutter and, together with any surface water, into the homes below. There were two open sewage pools in Highbury Place which gave off an awful smell, while in Clarence Place, sewage drained into huge cesspools directly underneath the houses.

The city corporation refused to have anything to do with Kingsdown or indeed Redland and Cotham because they were outside the city. As early as 1749 residents were complaining bitterly about the lack of sewers, police and street lights. Crime was rife in these unlit, unpatrolled areas and the *Bristol Intelligencer* reported in 1749: "Crowds of dissolute and disorderly persons have been entertained at about seven or eight unruly public houses near the gallows on St Michael's Hill and many insults and robberies committed on the market people and others travelling thereabout, but the gentlemen of that parish having bravely prosecuted and caused several penalties to be levied on the keepers of the houses, they are all routed away."

They weren't routed very far, however. In 1773, a petition was sent to the council from householders on St Michael's Hill and in Kingsdown complaining again that the unruly crowds who gathered for the public hangings on the hill were causing great damage to their homes. They wanted the gallows moved to Brandon Hill, but nothing was done.

The problem of cutpurses, high tobymen and burglars became so bad that in 1782, the residents of Kingsdown advertised "For a few able bodied men to be employed as a nightly patrol." The watch was maintained well into the last century but efforts to get street lighting failed until the great cholera outbreak of 1850 galvanised the council into action. Redland, Cotham and Kingsdown were rapidly provided with sewerage and, eventually, gas street lighting.

One of the best known meeting places in those early days was the Montague Tavern, a favourite place for duels and noted for its turtle soup. Live turtles would be brought up from the quay below and kept alive until needed. Another well known hostelry was the Trout Inn in Cherry Street off Stokes Croft which lasted from 1614 to its demolition in 1919. Boys from the nearby Stokes Croft Endowed School would call here for breakfast beer and in later years it became a favourite haunt of rugby players. The bowfronted window from the pub can still be seen at Blaise Castle Museum.

Kingsdown has suffered greatly this century, mainly from insensitive hospital development, blocks of flats which dwarf the Georgian houses and the encroachment of warehousing. But what is left is well worth saving and the majority of residents today understand and appreciate the area.

The area is rich in anecdotes such as the story of Dame Pugsley's Field (now Fremantle Square) where the widow of a Royalist officer was buried in 1705 in her wedding dress—60 years after her husband was killed by Roundheads. She was carried on an open bier

Above: St. Michael's Hill before the decline. **Opposite:** 1950s squalor. Rehabilitation was still some years off.

with music and girls scattering flowers and thousands of people attended the funeral.

St Michael's Hill was notorious for the gallows there, as recounted earlier. Those condemned to death had to walk from Newgate prison below and small children suffering from warts were held up to touch their bodies nine times in the belief that they would be cured. People would beg for the rope which was supposed to be a guaranteed medicine for numerous ailments. One hangman, William Curtis, wasn't much of an advertisement for capital punishment as a deterrent. He robbed a pedlar to add to his inadequate wages, was transported, but secretly returned two years later. Instead of moving quietly to an area where he wouldn't be known, he not only returned to Bristol but when he found the pedlar in Newgate on a debt charge, went daily to taunt him. Inevitably he was recognised and ended his life on the gallows where he had executed so many others.

Another St Michael's Hill character was George Pocock, a school teacher in the last century who built huge kites and harnessed them to his own design of kite carriage. With six passengers on board, his kite carriages managed 25mph on the Downs and the Pocock family travelled for years by these machines. Apart from not needing feeding, the kite carriages were also free from the tolls because no one could decide how they should be classified. Pocock's kites grew so big eventually that they could pull four carriages at once and he also sailed the Bristol Channel in a kite powered boat.

Then there was Samuel Seyers who ran Royal Fort boarding school and wrote a famous history of Bristol from manuscripts at the Bodleian Library in Oxford because Bristol council refused him access to their own archives.

St Michael on the Mount Without is close to the hill, a church where for more than 200 years huge sticky buns called Tuppenny Starvers have been handed out to children and Colston's alms-houses residents once a year. No one is quite sure how the practice began.

Cotham parish church played a large role in the history of the area under an earlier incarnation as Highbury Congregational Chapel. It was designed by the important Victorian church architect, William Butterfield, who was commissioned through his aunt, Mrs H O Wills of the tobacco family who were closely connected with the Congregational movement. Butterfield was 'high church' and was so disturbed by this tacit support of non-conformism that he refused to build churches for anyone but the established church from then on.

St Michael's Hill was the main roadway from Bristol to Aust ferry. Highbury Chapel was built close to the spot where, in the 16th century, five Protestants—William Shapton, Richard Sharp,

Edward Sharp, Thomas Hale and Thomas Bannion—were burned to death for refusing to accept what one chronicler described as "the unscriptured practices of the Roman Catholic church."

It was also the spot where the gallows stood, a place called Bewells, or Bueols, Cross. This was the boundary of the old city where several tracks met near a well and where an ancient Christian monument once stood, probably on the site of an even older pagan landmark. In 1829, historian William Tyson wrote to the *Bristol Mirror*: "In laying out the new road, now forming from the top of St Michael's Hill through the Gallows Field to Cotham, the fragment of the once venerated memorial to Christianity has been carelessly fractured and rudely thrown from the spot on which it has stood for ages." Part of Bueols Cross was saved and was incorporated in the new chapel although the local legend soon grew up that it was part of the gallows stone instead.

Highbury Chapel was started in 1824 when the land was bought by Richard Ash and given to the trustees. It was founded by members of Penn Street Tabernacle who also founded Arley Chapel, Kingsland Chapel and Anvil Street Chapel. "The sacred edifice," reported the *Bristol Mercury*, "will be reared in close proximity to the spot on which in darker times so often frowned the hideous tree of death. How many of the unhappy wretches who have terminated a miserable existence on this spot owed their ignominious end to the want of early instruction in the principles and truths of the gospels and a consequent neglect of the means of grace?" Victorians, even newspaper reporters, never missed a chance for a quick moral lecture.

The opening dinner was held at the Montague Tavern where the bill for 56 dinners, beer, coffee and waiters was four shillings per head and 16 bottles of sherry were drunk for £4.16s.

Chapel members started a school in Anglesea Place, Clifton which they ran until local councils took over all schools, but there was an extraordinary row when they wanted to open a cemetery next to the church. Nearby residents complained that there was a restriction of use on the land, namely that it should not be used for the trades of "an inn, or hotel keeper, slaughterman, butcher, tallow chandler, soap boiler, pipe maker, lime burner, ale house keeper, retail cider and beer house, blacksmith, or (and this was the important bit) any other trade deemed noisome or offensive to the neighbourhood." Legal opinion was sought and it was decided that a cemetery was not officially noisome or offensive, but only one child was ever buried there and the plan was quietly dropped.

The chapel was extended in 1862 by E W Godwin, a friend of Oscar Wilde and the painter Whistler, who was born in Old Market and had watched the original chapel being built from his classroom in Exton's School, Cotham New Road.

Colston's Girls' School, Cheltenham Road and St. Jude's National School, Wade Street.

He was keenly interested in the theatre, especially Shakespeare, designed dresses and scenery and also reviewed plays (very acidly) at the Theatre Royal. He met the young Ellen Terry there and invited her and her sister to playreading classes at his home. She was then 14 but seven years later Godwin and Ellen eloped and spent many happy years together. Godwin added a tower, lecture hall and organ space to Highbury, and an oak screen. It was all rather more C of E than congregationalist and led to an entertaining poem in which a Mrs St Mary Redcliffe asks a Mr St Michael: "The question that I want to ask (don't think the old girl is sour), Is whether we've got any chance against Highbury tower." Mr St Michael responded by expressing surprise at the screen, tower and stained glass windows ("Good gracious, those always were ours") and added: "Such inroads are tremendous. That place at Highbury on the hill cuts such shine above us unless you help us with goodwill our friends will cease to love us."

The best known minister of the chapel was the Rev David Thomas. When he died in 1875 after 31 years there, shops closed and crowds lined the funeral route. The new Bishopston Congregational church opened in 1878 was called David Thomas Memorial church. It was demolished, apart from the prominent tower, in the summer of 1986 to make way for sheltered accommodation for the elderly. The tower was given a new life as a lift shaft!

It was David Thomas' son, Rev Arnold Thomas who unwittingly drew the church into one of the most famous industrial disputes of the late Victorian years. A member of the congregation was a Mr Sanders who ran a sweet factory, employing many local women and girls at between 3s and 7s a week and with no "right of combination". Sanders sacked one girl and then 40 others and the rest went on strike. He promptly wrote to the local newspapers apologising to the public for the inconvenience cause by pickets and girls seeking contributions to the strike fund. "We have had no difficulty in filling the places of the poor victims who have thrown up their situations," he added. "Most excellent relations have hitherto existed between us and our work people."

Mr Thomas, who had taken over from his father, unwisely intervened by paying a surprise visit to Sanders' factory and interviewing girls still working there. "We met nowhere with any trace of dissatisfaction but were assured in every room with a warmth and unanimity that impressed us that there was no reasonable ground for complaint," he stated. "Charges brought against Mr Sanders are shamefully unjust."

The 104 girls by now on strike disagreed: so did many other church ministers and influential citizens, and Mr Thomas was forced to make a new statement. "I claim as truly as any clergymen to care for poor girls like these," he asserted. "I admit with some sorrow that their wages are miserably low. But I do not think it just to charge the perplexities and griefs of our complex social system to the account of any single employer who is himself subject to the painful pressure of it."

It didn't help. In November 1892, hundreds of girls and their supporters paraded to Highbury Chapel but were refused entry, so they held a public meeting nearby. The dispute fizzled out after Sanders agreed, magnanimously, to take back just six of the strikers "as evidence of good faith." He added: "In compliance with Mr Thomas' wishes and in the interests of peace, I am ready to make this concession." It did Mr Thomas' reputation much harm and even today there are grandchildren of the Sweet Girls who recall their grandmothers talking bitterly about the dispute.

But workers from Highbury did much good, too. Mrs Ellen Williams recalled in her old age working in the Ragged School in Leadhouse Lane in the slums of the city below. The children she taught were filthy and foul mouthed, dressed in old clothes tied with string and rarely removed for luxuries like a wash. They played her up cruelly until her father came down and thrashed the ringleaders. Each year Mrs Williams would take the children on an outing to Cotham (where Trelawney Road now stands) and later to Weston-super-Mare. Her main task there was stopping them getting too unruly, chasing the older ones out of the pubs and getting them all home again without too much sand or seaweed.

Highbury Chapel is now St Mary's, a Church of England, which would have pleased the original architect. It is particularly noted for a fine memorial to Arnold Thomas by Eric Gill, the type designer and artist, which is cut into a corbel descending from the roof. Arnold Thomas may not have been much good at industrial relations but he was thought of so highly by his congregation—including Mr Sanders no doubt—that they presented him with a fine coach and horses.

Nearby in Alfred Place is a memorial of a different kind. Conservationists worked hard in the 1970's to save some attractive houses from being demolished as part of the increasing depredations by the university and the hospital. A housing association converted a building into flats and on the side in bronze relief are the heads of bricklayers Ray Mitchell, Harry Brown and site foreman Steve Harris. The relief is by Stephen Joyce and a nice reminder of the medieval practice of including the faces of masons on cathedrals and churches.

Cotham is now only distinguishable from Kingsdown by the age and style of the houses. It is a grand area, full of large houses now happily being lovingly cared for and restored since the threat of an urban motorway down Cotham Brow receded.

The development of Kingsdown would have continued into

Traffic-free streets: Ashgrove Road, Horfield and Grosvenor Road, St. Pauls.

Sussex Place, 1958.

Cotham, but money ran out and it wasn't until 1839 that the real house building began. The spread of the area was rapid, despite the problems with policing, street lights and sewerage mentioned earlier. Cotham Lodge, a 17th century mansion was summarily demolished in 1846 and turned into a building site known as Cotham Park and all that remains of the houses are the two obelisks at the entrance of the road which marked the start of the mansion grounds.

Stephen Jones of Redland and Cotham Amenities Society summed up the appeal of the area in his definitive book on Cotham architecture, *Cotham Walks* (1980). "The hilltop has a double townscape character—prospect and aspect," he wrote. "From many parts of east and north Bristol, the horizon is dominated by the hillside strewn with villas crowned by the long horizontal of the Fremantle Road terraces, above which rises the tower of St Matthews. From the hill top, there are dramatic views over the north and east of Bristol."

Cheltenham Road divides Cotham from St Pauls and Montpelier on the other side. It contains Arley Chapel, now a Polish Roman Catholic church, built by the team of Foster and Wood who also designed part of Clifton's Victoria Square, Bristol Grammar School, the Grand Hotel, the first Colston Hall, Shepherds Hall, Old Market, and many other well-known Bristol buildings. The strangely striped, red and yellow Colston's Girls' School (once matched by a library across the road which was destroyed in the Blitz) was by William Venn Gough, who also designed the Cabot Tower. He may have had something to do with a pair of houses nearby in Effingham Road, St Andrews, called Colston House and Dolphin House, which were reportedly built for the head mistress and chaplain of the school and which reflect the design of the school building on a smaller, domestic scale. More likely it was a later architect who was asked to keep to the theme, but there are no records to settle the matter.

St Pauls was a parish carved from the parish of St James as the population grew on that side of the city. The church with its distinctive wedding cake tower was finished in 1794, just 500 yards from St James itself, but the new residents of fashionable Portland Square wanted their own church. Architect Mike Jenner says drily: "Snobbery was probably a major factor: a new church would put up house values." Daniel Hague, a former mason turned architect and developer, claimed he got the idea for the tower from the Royal Exchange in London. Hague is also credited with designing Portland Square which he named after the Duke of Portland, Lord High Steward of Bristol. The original contractors went bankrupt and the houses were unfinished until well into the 19th century but once completed it became a very fashionable area. It has fallen on hard times recently but, like neighbouring Brunswick Square, seems to have weathered the depression and is now being cared for and sympathetically restored.

York Street nearby was built in 1766 as the result of a City Improvement Act to link the Full Moon inn with Brunswick Square. The first section of road was called Cumberland Street, the second York Street, after the King's brothers.

Again, the boundaries have blurred in this old area and few could say where St Pauls ends and St Werburghs, St Agnes and St Judes begin.

But probably the most interesting story is that of St Werbergh's church. How many people today realise this church once stood in Small Street in the centre of the city? It was declared unsafe in 1757 and a nationwide appeal was launched to repair it. But the eastern end of the church blocked Small Street which was becoming one of the busiest streets in the city. In 1878, the church was demolished and rebuilt—although by no means exactly—in Mina Road. Parts of the church found their way into Arno's Court, which caused a minor scandal, and there were strong rumours that some of the stone was "lost" en route and later reappeared in a row of cottages.

St Jude's was another church built to serve an overcrowded district, this time carved from the parishes of Holy Trinity and SS Philip and Jacob. It was built on Poyntz Pool, once a local bull baiting ground where a bull was baited annually for the Aldermen's Feast on All Saints Day. The building was started in 1848 and completed in a year, to the fury of the local residents who presumably preferred the bull baiting. A centenary history of St Jude's published in 1949 recorded simply: "It was found necessary to protect the building in its earlier stages from the violence of the local population by erecting barricades." Mr Arthur Withers, People's Warden in 1949 and a parishioner for 60 years remembered the turn of the century: "There were many more houses in the parish and many overcrowded. Also a large number of lodging houses from which about 1,000 lodgers a week passed through the parish. There were many public houses and plenty of fighting at night and the police had a busy time. The proper St Jude's people were very respectable and very clean. I remember an old friend, a horse and cattle dealer, who lived in the parish and was very kind to St Jude's. Being asked why he did not come to church, his reply was: 'Because I tell so many lies.' "

Many older folk in St Jude's remember the Sisters of Charity who were based in Wade Street—Sister Clare who would "sally forth in a cart filled with baskets to beg food for her poor in Clifton" and Sister Bessie who served cooked dinners twice a week for a halfpenny and refused to divulge where the money came from to do it.

The Church that moved. St. Werburgh's Church in Corn Street, before demolition and reconstruction on its present East Bristol site.

St Simon's, Baptist Mills, was another parish subtracted from that of Holy Trinity and the foundation stone was laid on Waterloo day, 1846, with a terribly pompous speech by the Mayor. In those days Lower Ashley Road, Mina Road and Pennywell Lane were only lanes and Newfoundland Road did not exist. It was a market garden area with a population of 2,000 very poor people, but amazingly, this nondescript area was the scene of fierce religious riots at the beginning of this century.

For 25 years from 1882, when he was appointed by Gladstone, to 1907 when he resigned, the Rev Nevile Birkmyre was the priest. He was a very strong Anglo Catholic, and introduced many Catholic practices into what had been a fairly Protestant church. He was bitterly opposed, even by his own bishop, but refused to give in, even when licenses were refused to his curates and the church-wardens demanded to see the credentials of any guest preachers he invited. The opposition increased after he introduced the use of incense and on June 1, 1902, nearly 3,000 Protestants forced their way into the church while he was celebrating Mass. There were scenes of "uproar and disorder" to quote a report of the time, but Father Birkmyre (as he preferred to be called) "proceeded steadily with the service, all hostile demonstration passing unnoticed." He was also strong fundamentalist, opposing any kind of "modernism" and his decision to move on in 1907 was welcomed in many quarters. But he was also much loved by some, and he did abolish pew rents and pew doors, still a barrier to the very poor attending church even at the beginning of this century.

It has to be remembered that the church was the centre of community life until comparatively recently, particularly in poorer parishes where, until the Welfare State was introduced, it acted as a safety net, social centre, Citizen's Advice Bureau and soup kitchen. Brookland Methodist Church, Lower Ashley Road, was typical of the inner city churches whose role as lynchpin of the area has long since vanished.

Brookland was started by William Gibbons, Sunday School Superintendent at Wesley Chapel, Baptist Mills in 1888. He was an energetic man, tireless in his work for the church and in 1887, his Sunday School had a staggering 2,473 children and 137 teachers. Gibbons started a day school, and two mission rooms in the district, ran singing classes and a penny bank to help savings and even sold hymn books at reduced prices. But in 1887, what are only recorded as "difficulties" arose, and Gibbons and most of the Sunday School staff resigned. They started meeting at the Vestry Hall, Pennywell Road and the following year set up The Society of Brookland Church and Sunday Schools.

The new church bought the Gunter and White estates in Lower Ashley Road and although serious floods affected the building, it was opened in April 1889. Even the names of the contractors have been faithfully recorded: Summerhayes, masons; Bale and Westlake, Clifton, carpenters; Jennings of Pennywell Road, timber merchants; J Wilkins, plumber; Mr Brown, tiler and plasterer; Mr Winter, gas fittings; Mr Edbrook, smith; Parnell and Sons, seating; architects, Foster and La Trobe.

Brookland Gospel Temperance Society held the first meeting on the new site, using drying sheds by the side of the mill stream. A new infants school replaced these sheds, the money being raised by a rally in the Colston Hall at which Dr Talmedge of America was the speaker.

William Gibbons died suddenly in 1897 by which time the church was established in the neighbourhood. It ran a Sunday School with 2,685 scholars (1891) and Gibbons Penny Bank took an amazing £562.19s.11d in one year alone. There was a Young Men's Bible Class, a Senior Men's Bible Class, a Young Men's Sunday Morning Class, a choir, a Sisterhood, a Women's Missionary Auxiliary, a Girls Friendly Society, Band of Hope, Scouts, Cubs, Brownies, Rangers, Young Men's Institute (there must have been a lot of young men), a youth club and an amateur drama group. And, remember, this was just one church in the Ashley area.

Some of the older parishioners recorded their memories of Brooklands for its diamond jubilee in 1948 and it is a valuable record of the importance of the church in its community—a record which could be equalled by most active churches in the earlier years of this century.

The highlight of the year was the annual outing to Weston, only put off once during what the jubilee booklet describes as the "1939-45 upheaval," when the zoo was the alternative. But 1921 was a typical year. "The sun was shining brightly on the vast crowd gathered on Stapleton Road platform. Three long and crowded trains left at stated intervals. The scene in the Salvation Army Hall was an animated one, a small army of happy willing workers were busy from the moment of arrival until 5.45 when the last hungry one had been served. Two thousand, two hundred and five people had sat down at the tables or had received a bag of eatables at the door."

Mr John Priscott was president of the Young Men's Bible Class when the First World War broke out and he wrote to every member called up—some 1,342 letters, 194 parcels and 28 postal orders. How many of his class ever came back? It is not recorded.

The Brookland choir claimed to be the second in the city to sing Handel's Messiah, (Bristol Choral Society was the first) and apart from Mendelssohn's Elijah, its repertoire includes lesser known and long forgotten pieces such as Joseph; Christ and His Soldiers; The Haymakers; Esther; The Galilean, and Bethlehem. The choir had days out too, travelling to Burnham, Cheddar and Wells, Portishead and Clevedon by train or horsebrake. They would take a parcel of music for a sing-song after tea and one former member recalled: "Once we ventured as far as Brighton. Visiting these more sophisticated resorts we became shy of singing in public and got into the habit of reserving the sing-song for the homeward journey."

The Girls Friendly Society started during the First World War, knitting socks, scarves and gloves for the troops but it gave many hundreds of girls a chance to learn the skills of cooking, needlework, embroidery, rug making, leatherwork and even millinery, "where we learned to make old hats look like new". The GFS also took members for a week or a fortnight at Winscombe, ran a savings bank, and a clothing club where the girls were able to buy all kinds of goods. Many older members also recall Brookland Happy Evenings, concerts with a temperance theme which eventually lost out to newer attractions like the picture theatres, and the Brookland Players who tackled everything from Shakespeare to Peg o' my Heart. The chapel screened one of the earliest talking pictures in 1935 (Lax of Poplar) and delighted in recording obscure facts—606 eggs were received on June 23, 1918 at an Egg and Flower Service; the electric light was switched on for the first time after the sermon on September 5, 1920; the tea for children of the unemployed on February 3, 1922. Like so many other churches, Brooklanders tried to practice what was preached.

Nearby in St Werburghs was Watercress Farm and in Victorian times pony traps would take picnic parties there each summer and on Bank Holidays. There would be gingerbread wafers and watercress sandwiches from the local beds. The brook which served the farm still runs through Ashley Hill in a tunnel by the railway embankment but the Green's Mills which it served have long gone. It was the spring on Ashley Hill that provided much of the water for old Bristol via the Quay Pipe, one of the principal conduits into the city. The water often failed to flow, usually because of dead cats blocking the pipe.

Ashley today is dominated by the buildings of the Muller Orphanages, now a technical college. Latimer, the annalist, described the Muller operation as "the most remarkable charity of which the city and indeed the Kingdom can boast."

George Muller was a Prussian who came to Britain as a missionary with the Society for the Conversion of the Jews. He arrived in Bristol in 1832 to become minister of Gideon Independent Chapel, Newfoundland Street, and two years later formed the Scriptural Knowledge Institution, with the aims of educating the poor and caring for orphan children. His first orphanage for 30 girls was in Wilson Street, St Pauls, followed by a second house for infants and a third—again in the same street—for boys. They were run on faith,

Horfield Rectory and Muller Orphanage.

Zoo outing for Muller orphans.

hope and charity, often with cash or food for only 24 hours ahead, but as the reputation of Muller's work spread, so donations began to arrive from all over the world. A fourth house was opened in Wilson Street but two large gifts persuaded Muller to buy seven acres on Ashley Hill at a discount price of £120. In June 1849, the children moved in, even though Muller was still relying on gifts to finance the project. Two extra buildings were erected in 1857 and 1862 and two more in 1868 and 1870. The total cost of the orphanage—£115,000. Donations in one year—(1868)—£700,000. By May 1886, nearly 7,300 children had been entrusted to Muller's orphanages, yet not once did he ever incur a debt which could not be met. Many people alive today are grateful to the Muller homes and many others remember the Muller girls parading in their bonnets and shawls.

The slopes of Montpelier were already settled by the time Muller started his work. The area was named after the place in southern France because it, too, was a place on a hill with a beautiful view.

It was a popular spot for outings with fine views, just the place for the new middle classes, and by the end of the 18th century the area was already being built up. The street names reflect the heroes of the time—like Picton Street after Captain Picton who in 1783 quelled an army mutiny on College Green and went on to become a general under Wellington, himself commemorated in Wellington Place.

Henry Broadribb, a junior warehouse clerk, lived in Wellington Place before he changed his name and found fame on stage as Henry Irving, while Picton Street was the home of Archie Leach, better known today as Cary Grant, who attended (and was expelled from) Fairfield Grammar School.

Bath Buildings commemorates Montpelier's biggest attraction, Rennison's Grand Pleasure Bath and Gardens. Territt's snuff mill was here, by a fine pond which was used for swimming, and in 1746 thread maker Thomas Rennison decided to buy the site for a scheme he hoped would make his fortune. At this time Montpelier was outside the city boundary and free from tiresome by-laws. Rennison advertised his premises as a Grand Pleasure Bath and Gardens and indeed the original pool was over 400ft in circumference. Rennison added a smaller pool for ladies, a bowling green, tea gardens, coffee house, and a tavern, the Old England. He offered concerts and slightly less cultured events like the drunken feasts where a mock mayor, sheriff and other dignitaries were elected. According to a newspaper cutting preserved in the Old England, the pub was responsible for reviving the ancient game of quoits in the area.

Only the pub remains today from Rennison's splendid scheme. The bath and gardens were a major attraction for more than a century but by 1916 their day was over. Four years later Colston's Girls'

School bought the bath and roofed it over as a warehouse, itself replaced in 1978 when Montpelier Health Centre was built. But there is a sunken recreation area at the rear of the school which has always been known as The Pleasaunce and it is possible that this is also a survivor from the great days of the Grand Pleasure Gardens.

Montpelier was also the setting for a most peculiar sect claiming to revive the old monastic order of St Benedict. It was started by a man called Lyne in 1864 in Trenchard Street but his alleged Benedictine services were so eccentric that on occasions the police had to be called. Two of the brothers tried to take a service while drunk and had to be forcibly removed and the brothers would hold noisy candlelit processions through the streets late at night. After numerous scandals, Lyne, or Brother Ignatius as he called himself, excommunicated the prior of the order, a man called Dundas or Brother Cyprian. Cyprian promptly formed a breakaway order in Montpelier where he built a chapel, started a home and a newspaper.

But, as reports of the time record, his unusual way of doing things attracted a wild and profligate bunch of 'worshippers' which led to many unedifying scenes (quite what happened isn't clear). In the end, the iron chapel was given to the vicar of Bedminster and in 1872 cash problems forced the Montpelier centre to close.

A religious row of a different nature lies behind the growth of Bishopston, a rather amorphous area which straddles the Gloucester Road. It was obviously prime building land once Cotham and Montpelier were built up but it was then part of the manor of Horfield over which the Bishop of Gloucester and Bristol had virtually feudal rights.

The bishop, Dr James Monk, offered to sell his interests for £11,587 with half the proceeds going to his family and half towards improving the livings of poor parsons. The complexity of the situation led to debates in Parliament with doubts over the legal status of the bishop's holdings as well as the rights of leaseholders and copyholders on the estate. While this was going on, no development could take place.

Dr Monk seems to have been a well meaning man who tried to thread his way through the ancient laws of lease and copyholding as best he could. But the £545 a year income from the manor attracted the interest of the Rev Henry Richards, perpetual curate of Horfield, who tried to persuade Parliament that Dr Monk had no right to sell the Horfield lease.

Richards was the largest copyholder and Dr Monk revealed he had managed to negotiate a lease for the manor which would have made him lord as well and the recipient of that useful £545 a year. Richards was furious that the bishop refused to accept his claim and, wrote Dr Monk, "his indignation exhibited itself in railing against his bishop". Dr Monk was eventually confirmed as the leaseholder and in 1858 a board of trustees took it over. "With the emancipation of the district from the copyhold system dates its rise and rapid growth as a suburb," recorded John Latimer.

But Richards was not finished. He agreed to the formation of a new parish in Horfield to be called Bishopston and for the bishop to be the patron. But after Dr Monks' death, he backed down, claiming he would never allow a Low churchman to nominate a clergyman in his parish. Richards had his eye on the value of the living, which was increasing in Bishopston was developed. He offered to build a church and endow it, provided the patronage was vested in him and his heirs. But the trustees now administering the manor of Horfield persuaded the new bishop to refuse Richards' offer, to his great fury. On June 20, 1858 the new church of St Michael and All Angels was opened on what is locally still called Pigsty Hill. The parish included parts of Horfield, Stapleton and St Andrews.

Bishopston, the suburb, started with Berkeley and Egerton Roads, handsome tree-lined streets built in what appeared to be orchards stocked with mature trees, many of which still survive today. There is a persistent story handed down in the area that no house in Berkeley Road was to be built under £650 and none in Egerton Road under £450 and that no pairs of houses were to be identical. It is impossible to say if it is true after more than a century, but there is still an astonishing diversity in house design and decoration.

There is little to be seen today of the green fields that once lined Gloucester Road as late as the turn of the century, yet, even as late as 1874, the area was so sparsely populated that two small boys walking from Stokes Croft to Horfield got lost. The older gave his coat to the younger and died of the cold overnight. He is commemorated in a stained glass window in Horfield church.

There was to have been a grand pleasure garden in Bishopston, another money-making scheme backed by the Rev Henry Richards. He sold Bristol Pleasure Garden Company eight acres of market gardens for £2,000 and they were laid out for public recreation. There was a big opening fete but for some reason the gardens never became popular and the site was eventually sold to the council for what is now Horfield prison.

Like many older areas, Bishopston is changing as more young families move in and renovate the old houses. The trend started in the early sixties when the big ambition to leave the city centre and move into semis in Yate or Whitchurch began to change. In 1967, the then vicar of Bishopston was able to state: "I began to get pretty depressed about the way the parish was getting depleted, but recently there has been quite a change. People have been moving in to the district and proving these old houses are capable of being adapted for modern living. I have been quite amazed at the way some young couples have completely redecorated these large houses in a most tasteful style."

Bishopston has its surprises like Princes Place, a tiny cul-de-sac tucked away behind the Gloucester Road shops. Alfred Hartnell built a row of cottages by a duckpond more than 160 years ago and his descendants still live there.

Nearby is Morley Square, a pleasant little oasis once destined as a car park. The central garden was under threat after the war for the railings had gone for the war effort, the coping stones had been knocked down and two air raid water tanks squatted on the grass.

Mr John Watts of No 17 saved the square almost single-handed. He collected £10 from each of the residents to have the tanks removed and filled in the hollows left and reseeded them. He also started a Morley Square preservation committee to keep the square looking trim and tidy.

St Andrews Park a few streets away was opened in 1897 on the site of an old ash tip, and cost £8,500. The bowling green there was turfed with grass from the coast between Avonmouth and Severn Beach and the park is one of the most delightful and restful in this part of Bristol.

Calico, Creosote and Colliers

Pat Smith and Martin J Powell recreate the hard life and close-knit communities in East Bristol.

Two well marked tracks wound away from Bristol's city walls in the Middle Ages. One climbed through the manor of Barton, skirting the hill which rose gently from the River Avon, passing through the forbidding Forest of Kingswood, and on to London.

The other, a much pleasanter path, meandered along the damp and verdant valley of the Frome River and on to Gloucester.

In those early days it was a brave man who set out to make these journeys—either on foot or by horse. But as the population of Bristol grew so did the need to make use of these fertile lands beyond the city wall.

By the sixteenth century Bristol was a prosperous trading centre, the second richest city in England, but these two important routes were in a shocking condition. In 1565 the city chamberlain ordered repair work to be carried out on "all the causeways seven miles every way about the city". Then in the 17th century their existence was acknowledged in written records. They were officially called the London Waye and the Gloucester Waye, and extremely busy highways they were, even in those early days of the city's development.

In 1765 a census of traffic showed that nearly two thousand vehicles and more than twelve thousand horses passed through Lawford's Gate.

Those travelling to London would have passed the hamlet of Barton Hill—a quiet, pastoral scene, just a few cottages huddled together and a sprinkling of larger houses standing in pleasant gardens. A lane wound from Pile Marsh through the hamlet to the glass houses and foundries of The Dings.

On the right, fields rose high from the road while to the left, the orchards and gardens of Easton and Whitehall provided goods for the city dwellers. This was a well used road and by 1800 there were places of entertainment, like Sarah Drewitt's fine house and gardens. Further on was the King's Arms, a popular stop for horse-drawn coaches and their thirsty travellers.

For those travelling to Gloucester and Oxford there were three coaching inns in the vast parish of Stapleton in the 1770's. The Full Moon, in the hamlet of Fishponds, was only a few yards from the old water-filled quarries, which gave the area its name. In the village of Stapleton itself there was a choice of The Bell or The Mason's Arms.

Frenchay was already a sizeable village by this time. The Manor House was built by wealthy Quakers around 1736 and other members of this religious order moved out from the city. They built their gracious homes from local materials.

East Bristol played its part in the local economy, with market gardens appearing in the lush valley of the River Frome. Fast streams carried water down the valley sides into the river and it wasn't long before these were also harnessed to provide energy.

There were several dozen water mills operating in the Bristol area and most of them were used for grinding corn. Mills grew up along the Frome Valley, with no less than eight recorded in the area between Eastville Park and Frenchay.

The best known, and best preserved today, is Snuff Mills. Despite its name it is unlikely that snuff was ever ground there and much of what visitors see today is a reconstruction. The fly wheel of a steam engine is also on show—this was used later to provide extra power to keep the mill operating. The original Snuffy's Jack Mill was, in fact, about half a mile upstream from the mill than can now be seen. All that remains today are just some irregularities in the ground.

Underneath the ground was an even more valuable asset—coal. That was to lead to industry developing that would change East Bristol for ever. The Great Vein ran underneath Bristol East and the demand for coal continued to grow from the end of the 18th century and throughout the 19th century. About the middle of the 18th century the first local pits were opened, grouped together under one manager. The industry expanded all over the area until this century, but the final decline came just before the Second World War as the coal seams were by then unecomonical.

At Staple Hill, Mr Shepherd's Works was one of the most successful pits as here the Great Vein and another seam of coal alongside gave a 12 foot thick layer of coal for the men to dig.

The New Level Works at Soundwell was also very productive and all the pit props and timber used to shore up the workings were cut nearby—a fact remembered to this day in the name Chiphouse Road.

The pitmen of East Bristol were a tough breed, determined to get their own way. Their tough and uncompromising way of life took over the green valleys and the earliest miners were described by one chronicler as "bare-headed, bare-legged, filthy ruffians". They worked hard and they certainly played hard with traditional rest activities of drinking and fighting.

In 1727 the authorities put up a toll booth at Fire Engine Gate near Fire Engine Farm. (The farm survives today, better known as St George's Park.) They had had experience of the colliers before, and feared that they would not pay the penny toll. So the rules said that only a ha'penny should be paid on a horse-load of coal, although a penny was charged for all other horse loads.

The miners were having none of it. On the first day they destroyed not only the Fire Engine Gate but all the other toll gates for miles around. The authorities put up new gates and these were also burnt down by the pitworkers. A year later the authorities were so fed up with the constant battle with the miners that they passed a new Act exempting coal from any charge.

An amusing example of the lawlessness of miners in the area was reported in *The Times* in April 1795.

"Monday last two bailiffs' followers made a seizure for rent at a house in Kingswood, near Bristol," it recorded. "An alarm being given, they were surrounded by a number of colliers, who conveyed them to a neighbouring coal-pit, and let them down, where they were suffered to remain till about 2 the next morning, when they were had up and, each having a glass of gin and some gingerbread given him, were immersed again in the dreary bowels of the earth, where they were confined, in all nearly 24 hours. On being released they were made to pay a fine of 6s 8d each for their lodging, and take an oath never to trouble, or molest, any of them again."

Those early miners of Kingswood forest certainly came in for criticism from a church organist in the area. He wrote: "It might have been thought that the ecclesiastical authorities of these parishes would have made some arrangement to meet the religious needs of the people who herded in the huts that stood among the black heaps of the forest.

"The colliers' children however, grew up in practical heathenism. As for the colliers themselves, they seemed to be beyond the reach of Christian influence. They formed a population that displayed every vice that disfigured the England of the eighteenth century. They were ignorant, violent, brutal, blasphemous, drunken, criminal.

"They were the terror of Bristol, as when work was scarce and bread was dear the whisper that the Kingswood colliers were on the march to the city caused a shudder among the shopkeepers, and stirred the civic authorities into wild activity."

One of the reasons for the reputation of the miners was that they led a hard, underpaid life at a time when their industry was expanding rapidly and profitably.

In 1801 Samuel Whittuck inherited his father's pits, including Staple Hill and Soundwell. He gave a great impetus to coal production in the area at a time when demand for fuel was growing from new industries.

Many large land owners in the area made fortunes from coal but most of the working colliers suffered great poverty in those early days. In 1821, one in every eight residents of St George was receiving parish relief—money given to the poorest people. A collier's weekly wage was around 10 shillings.

But not all the colliery bosses were ruthless exploiters. Handel Cossham, for instance, became the owner of two large collieries in the 19th century and he was one of the most humane employers. Cossham was a self-taught geologist and was well-known for his religious and educational work in the area. He helped to found a school for the children of the colliers in Staple Hill, and at one time his pits provided work for 1,500 men.

The movement of coal also led to the development of the railway in the area. A horse tram road, running from the Floating Harbour to Coalpit Heath became the Bristol and Gloucester Railway. A new line ran through Staple Hill, Fishponds and St Philips, and had extensions to Lawrence Hill. It was bought by the Great Western Railway company in 1845.

By 1879 smaller collieries had grown up in the area, including those owned by Leonard and Boult in Easton and Hanham. The Easton pit was the scene of an explosion in 1886. There were 250 men trapped down the pit and five men lost their lives.

East Bristol was, by then, a real mining community with pits dotted throughout the area. Those in Soundwell, three in all, were closed around 1850. Others in Hanham kept working much later. In 1878 Leonard and Boult bought the Whittuck estate and became the owners of the Hanham pits, which included Shot Patch Pit, near Mount Hill Brickworks and one on Jefferies Hill.

In 1890 Handel Cossham died. Parkfield colliery and his other pits were sold off to build a hospital which was named after him. The new owners, The East Bristol Colliery Company, eventually closed the last pit in 1936, when just 180 men were still employed.

One pit in Hanham opened and closed this century. It was off Memorial Road and opened in 1906 and closed in 1926. Horses were used to haul coal and were brought up to graze in the fields nearby.

The arrival and disappearance of the mines had certainly left its mark. East Bristol was now filled with street after street of small houses. Many were built to house Cossham's employees; some for railwaymen, and others, in the Easton area, for the men that worked the Easton Pit near St Gabriel's Church from 1881 to 1911.

The growth of East Bristol and other suburbs around the city led to numerous attempts during the 19th century to extend the city boundary. People were living outside the jurisdiction of the city and the corporation was beginning to realise that it was losing out on rates and that East Bristol was no longer countryside but, increasingly, an extension to the city. In 1835, a commission considered the boundaries of Bristol and a further 3,706 acres were enclosed. These included the popular areas of St Philip and Jacob.

By 1868 Bristol wanted to extend its boundaries again—this time to include St George. A fight against this began and the expansion was over-ruled by parliament. But the idea did not go away and by 1894 there was a new move to include another 21,000 acres in the city boundary, including St George, Stapleton and Fishponds. This met with even tougher opposition as St George and Stapleton had become urban district councils the previous year. Officials in St George pointed out that they could provide better facilities than Bristol.

Both areas had their own school boards and St George had gone ahead with new school buildings and boasted a higher standard of education than could be found in the city. They could also boast a public park, and a well-maintained cemetery. Stapleton argued that it had its own fire-fighting equipment and an isolation hospital.

But the protests this time were to little avail. In 1897 a major boundary extension took place and Stapleton and St George, some 7,036 acres, became part of the city.

The creation of the Floating Harbour in Bristol and the digging of the Feeder canal linking the city docks with East Bristol made East Bristol attractive to industries in the 19th century. Barton Hill, which had been a few scattered cottages and houses, was to change beyond recognition and become the centre of a thriving cotton industry.

The Great Western Cotton factory became the focal point of the area for the next century and led to many houses being built for the workers. Cotton cloth had been manufactured in Bristol from 1793 in Temple Street but this factory had closed down.

In the spring of 1837 a group of ten influential businessmen, in conjunction with Mr G B Clarke of Manchester, revived the idea and formed a private company called Clarke, Acramans, Maze and Company. A year later this became the Great Western Cotton Company and a piece of land was bought at Barton Hill. On April 18, 1837 a foundation stone was laid to mark the site of the intended factory. A year later, a fête took place to mark the completion of the factory and the first piece of cotton was presented to the mayor, Mr Haberfield, in January 1839.

One poetic account of the factory, by historian William Sanigar, written in the 1950's said: "Swiftly then flew the shuttles in the mill, and ere many months calico equal to that of Manchester was being dispersed over England. And soon from the landing stage on the Feeder sturdy little ships laden with cotton twist slipped out to the open sea.

"Dropping a part of their cargo at Gibraltar they rounded Spain and made for the northernmost shore of Italy. From Genoa they sailed down the western coast, discharging at Leghorn and Messina. Nosing their way through the straits they turned into the Adriatic, passed along the eastern coast of Italy to Ancona, and then on to Venice. Having thus girdled Italy round about with the products of Barton Hill they crossed the gulf to Trieste and trimmed their sails for the western isles of Greece where they called at Corfu, and then made for Malta, where the last load was dropped."

The Great Western Cotton Factory (now demolished) gave work to 2,000 people at the height of its prosperity and turned a quiet country area into a bustling suburb.

The Feeder canal had certainly become the gateway to the world but life was far from romantic for the workers in the mill. At its height the factory gave work to 2,000 people and turned a quiet country area into a bustling city suburb.

Churches, shops and pubs were built to cater for the community and although the face of the area has changed since the factory went into liquidation in 1925, it has left a legacy in the street names today. Great Western Lane, named after the factory, and Aiken Street, named after Peter Aiken, one of the original founders, are just two examples.

The workers were crammed into terraced houses and the shifts in the factory began at 5.30am and did not end until 5.30pm. Many people were ill from working in the humid conditions where they ate their lunch squeezed in the aisles between machines. Wages were low with a woman worker getting just over 4s a week. Many, who could cope with the machinery, worked more than one loom so that they could take home a better wage.

Although conditions were bad the weaving girls always looked clean in their white aprons, with pockets for equipment. If anyone died they held a unique collection where a girl would stand by the factory gate with her calico apron held out for her colleagues to drop coins in for the family as they left the factory.

The factory became so well known that in Bristol many people referred to Barton Hill as the cotton mills. Other factories grew up to make use of the shipping along the Avon after the Feeder canal opened.

In 1843 Isambard Kingdom Brunel wanted a material to preserve the sleepers on the Great Western Railway. He decided on creosote and it was on the banks of the Avon that he built a distillery. The foreman in charge of the distillery was Mr William Butler and from that modest beginning he built up a huge plant serving six counties. The smelly, unpleasant factory, popularly known as the tar works, nestled in a pretty valley known as Crew's Hole, near the junction of the Feeder and the Avon.

The area was originally known as Scruize Hole and many people have waxed lyrical about its beauty. It remains as a splendid wooded valley even today.

One traveller described it like this in a guide to walks in the area: "Not unexpected on a storm-bound coast, it yet would stir us to admiration; but here far inland, 'tis with a catch of the breath that strangers mark this cliff upflung against the sky.

"Then strange it is that men who know it well should pass unseeing and unmoved, though no parish surely has its fellow for many a mile around. Might one give it a second name it has never before received but richly deserves? What more fitting than the Miniature Clovelly of the West."

But if Crew's Hole was a little beauty spot, it was rapidly being surrounded by a tide of factories as the industrial revolution went at full pace in Bristol.

In 1851 the Bristol Wagon Works was built at Lawrence Hill. It employed 900 people in its heyday and did not close until 1923. At Crew's Hole, the Netham Chemical works opened in 1859 and the area around was described as having a "hard, grimy reality". Huge mounds of raw material for the factories were transported on the river and the Feeder canal.

Closely packed, back-to-back houses gradually grew up to accommodate the workers, filling what was once countryside. A field of rhubarb was cleared for more homes and the nearby pub was named the Rhubarb Tavern to commemorate it. Conditions changed little right up until the 1920's, and many older residents of the area remember what life was like. Most of the people who lived in the back-to-back houses at Barton Hill shopped locally and made use of the four grocers, two chemists, hardware shop and butchers. It was common to see pigs herded through the streets to the back of the butchers, where they were slaughtered.

Mice were always a problem and sanitation usually consisted of outside toilets, sometimes shared, and a tin bath in front of the fire. One man, who was a chemist in Beaufort Road before the First World War, also filled the role of local doctor and local vet. He was frequently knocked up at midnight by anxious locals wanting pills and potions to revive ailing horses. They needed to have the horse on his feet by the morning if they were to earn a living.

His son remembers: "People came from miles around to see dad. Some from Brislington and St Anne's. He was one of the few people that could read and they would bring things to him for him to read to them and ask his advice. He was in a small rank of shops and had a nice little walled garden at the back where he kept some chickens. The people in Beaufort Road formed their own close-knit society."

By the 1920's, entertainment had arrived in the form of the cinema. The Globe at Lawrence Hill, built around 1910, was the traditional Saturday morning destination for dozens of children, who sat on hard wooden forms to watch flickering black and white images for 1d.

Churches also played a major part in the social life of the area. At Stapleton the church was at the centre of an unholy row in the 1850's because it was too small. Dr James Henry Monk, the Bishop of Gloucester and Bristol, sent a letter to the churchwardens of the parish in April 1854 saying he would rebuild the church at his own expense. The letter was sent from Stapleton Palace, formerly Stapleton House, which is now Colston's School.

He described the church at that time as "mean in structure and of inadequate capacity". The motive behind his offer was to put an end

Top: Eastville Park, 1905, and everyone wearing a hat. **Bottom:** less formal boating on the lake in the 1950s.

to chronic quarrels over pews and to provide accommodation for the poor. In order to ensure there was room for the poor, he said his family would not have a seat reserved.

But Mr J H Greville Smyth said he would oppose the demolition of the old church unless his rights in the chancel, including the selling or letting of pews, was acknowledged. The difficulty was resolved by a typical English compromise. The old chancel remained and the new church was built around it. Bishop Monk died in June 1856 before the new church was consecrated. Among his last acts were the gift of an organ and a clock to the church. The church had cost him over £5,000.

But it was not so much the fabric of the church as the life of the church, providing social centres, clubs and entertainment throughout the area, which is remembered by the people who lived in the area. Non-conformist chapels spread rapidly with Kensington Baptist Church in Stapleton Road among the most popular. The large church of St Ambrose in Whitehall Road, with its imposing southern tower, earned the nickname of the cathedral of East Bristol. The religious life of Victorian Bristol was vigorous and that vigour spilled over into the first part of this century with Sunday schools packed with children and many social events revolving around the church and its officials.

The Redfield Wesleyan Chapel and Sunday School in Church Road became a focus for the working class people in that area from the beginning of the 19th century. From the 1800's onwards, there was an annual Sunday School treat every Whit Monday. On that day the pupils would go to Farmer Veale's Farm on the St Anne's side of the Avon, near what was later to become the board mills.

One former Sunday School pupil recalled: "The programme for this red letter day in our Sunday School life was as follows: the first duty of the teachers and officers was to attend a prayer meeting at 6am, there to ask for fine weather and for protection against harm and accident for all those taking part in the day's festivities.

"After this, various members of the staff proceeded to cut up bread and butter and cake, while others packed a portion of each in paper bags; each bag containing sufficient food for a scholar. Others assisted in loading vans with seats for the accommodation of adult visitors to the field, tables, urns for preparing tea, the aforesaid bags of food, ginger beer, sweets and all the other necessaries for assuring the comfort and enjoyment of the children, their parents and friends.

"At or about 11am the children with their teachers formed in classes around the chapel, and at a given signal proceeded in order of seniority to the river bank at Crew's Hole, where barges were waiting to transport them to the farm on the opposite side.

"A senior scholar with assistance (very necessary on a breezy day)

Toys and household utensils being made and enamelled at University Settlement.

carried the school banner at the head of the procession.

"At this date no bridges spanned the river at any point between Keynsham and Day's Lock Bridge, and there was no public access to the Somerset side of the river. Hence the necessity for marine transport. The voyage across the river was naturally very short; but sufficient time was always found wherein the scholars gave full force and vent to the singing of the nautical hymn, "We Are Out on the Ocean Sailing".

The Sunday School trip changed slightly when Farmer Veale moved to another farm at Londonderry, near Keynsham. On that longer journey up river, one boat got stuck in the mud and the other pupils hooted with derision as they sailed past.

In time the annual boat trip to Farmer Veale's field ended and the more traditional Sunday School outing to the seaside replaced it.

The great Labour politician, Ernest Bevin, was a prominent member of St Mark's Baptist Church in Easton in his formative years. The man who went on to become Foreign Secretary, made some of his first public speeches as a lay preacher with the church. Bevin was baptised at the age of 18 and astounded many of his fellow church companions with his knowledge and power of speech, even as a teenager. His first address at one meeting consisted of a 30 minute talk on the history of Israel.

One woman went up to him afterwards and asked: "Where did you get all that from, Ernest?" He replied: "By staying up late at night to study." He often gave Saturday night open-air sermons in the area and was a sidesman for the church, visiting those who wanted to join. Another task carried out by Bevin was the distribution of harvest festival gifts from the church to Muller's orphanage.

His later aspirations were clearly shown when he started a Right to Work committee, which demanded work or maintenance for the unemployed. The city council took little notice until Bevin organised a dramatic protest to draw their attention. He marshalled the unemployed one Sunday morning at the Horsefair and they marched to the Cathedral where they sat quietly at the back during a service and then filed out in absolute silence at the end of the sermon. When the council saw the ragged group in their parade they feared a riot, and were so impressed with their conduct that they set about finding employment for the men.

The Baptist church had started in Easton in 1897 with 40 people who broke away from the Kensington Fellowship. For the first few years of this century, they were trying to raise cash to build their own place of worship. One story at the time concerned the fund-raising efforts of one of the church's founding fathers, Mr H Wyatt. He is said to have gone to Mr Hill's greengrocery shop in Eastville and asked if there was anything he would give towards a forthcoming fund-raising bazaar. Mr Hill replied: "I'll give you a sack of potatoes if you can get them home." Mr Wyatt accepted that challenge and left the shop with an enormous bag. It was not long before he had to put them down as they weighed so much. Just then a woman passed by pushing a pram with a crying baby in it. Mr Wyatt stopped her and offered to carry the baby and comfort it if she would put the potatoes in the pram. She agreed to this arrangement and the potatoes were safely delivered to the fund-raising stall.

During the fund-raising, the deacons at the church made a pact that wherever they were and whatever they were doing, every day at 12 noon they would stop and pray for the success of the building scheme. The church was eventually opened for the first time on November 22, 1911.

With rows of houses now filling the land nearest the city, and all the new factories, the developers started moving further east. Horse-drawn trams speeded this development by enabling people living further out to get into town for work and shopping.

In June 1876, the Tramway Company opened a line from Old Market to Eastville. In September this was linked through Broadmead to provide journeys right across Bristol from East to West. By October the line had been extended to St George and a horse-bus feeder service took passengers in to Kingswood.

The horse-drawn trams proved expensive and slow. Horses travelled at 6 miles per hour and worked four hours a day. As the network grew larger there were 300 horses operating in Bristol and the service was becoming uneconomic. Running costs for a horse tram were estimted at 9d a mile.

Tramway operators were looking around for easier ways to operate their network of public transport in Bristol and were casting envious eyes at the steam trains travelling along on the Great Western Railway. It just happened that at the same time, the Bristol engineering firm of Fox and Walker were building six steam tram engines for Rouen in France. The authorities decided to try one out on the streets of Bristol to see if they were practical.

In the early hours of December 4, 1877, 40 VIPs boarded a horse-car pulled by a steam engine at Eastville depot. The operation was carried out at night so as not to frighten horses that might be on the route during the day. The VIPs went through Old Market but the engine would not pull them up the hill by Bristol Royal Infirmary. A report in the *Bristol Times and Mirror* at the time said: "No amount of coaxing would persuade it beyond this point so it was driven out to St George instead, amid much smoke and steam".

The steam engines were sent to Rouen and it was November 1880 before steam trams were introduced in parts of Bristol. Then they were only used on lines to Horfield and were phased out within a

Tramway Junction, Eastville.

92

year as being uneconomical and unpopular with passengers.

In the 1890's the answer to a cheaper and more efficient tram service was found to be electricity. Poles started to appear between Old Market and Lawrence Hill to carry the electric wires and a powerhouse was built alongside the tramcar sheds in Beaconsfield Road, St George. The electric trams were to link Bristol and Kingswood and there was such public excitement at the prospect that the trials had to be held in secret at night.

One report recorded: "So keen were the residents on the subject of electric traction that some circumspection was needed in order to make the first run in comparative quiet. It was made shortly after midnight. The good people of Bristol had scarcely entered into their first sleep when a glaring light streaked across the bedroom windows. They realised the company was stealing a march on them; up went windows and out went heads and there was the first car gliding down the street. That part of Bristol that was traversed by the electric cars immediately got up and waited for the return of the surreptitious car. Never was an electric car awaited in this country by a scantier clad concourse."

On Monday October 14, 1895, factories and schools in East Bristol closed for half a day as the trams were to make their first runs. At 12.30pm eight tram cars left Old Market and set off towards Kingswood. They were decorated with flags and shields and were cheered through the streets by the crowds. The first car, numbered 89, carried Mr William Butler, chairman of the directors, Mr George White, managing director, the city High Sheriff and Mr Eugene Griffin of the General Electric Company of America.

Councillors from St George and Kingswood and members of the press were in the second tram driven by Mr Clifton Robinson. Mr Butler made a speech to the cheering crowds at Kingswood and then the party returned, pausing briefly for a tour around the power house at St George, and were taken by horse and carriage from Old Market for a slap-up meal and celebration in the Grand Hotel.

But the Tramways Company made sure that the celebrations did not exclude the ordinary people of the area. It provided money for 1,200 aged and poor people in Kingswood and St George to have a "meat dinner". Church leaders throughout the area organised the feasts with a newspaper at the time reporting that 1,250lbs of meat, 280lbs of cake, 900 buns and scones, 70lbs of sugar and 130 gallons of milk and tea were consumed. The guests then sat down to an entertainment presided over by the Rev E D Green of Bethesda Chapel, Redfield, before being sent on their way with free tickets for a ride on the trams.

The electric system was extended again on February 1, 1897, from West Street, Old Market, along Trinity Road, into Stapleton Road and out to Eastville. At that time the journey from Old Market to

Rural peace at Frenchay. The village plays a county team at the start of the 1950 season.

Kingswood took 32 minutes with a fare of 3d. The trams had the letter "K" for Kingswood on them and carried a yellow light on the front at night.

People did not only travel on the trams for work. They also used them for getting to the many places where Bristolians spent their leisure hours. One such place was the Quaker village of Frenchay.

Frenchay was formerly known as Fromeshaw, which changed in the course of time to Franshawe, Franchehay and finally the present day spelling. This means "the copse on the River Frome". Frenchay Common originally stretched from Frenchay and Pearces Hill, along the river and over to the old Gloucester Road. Building eroded it gradually but from 1846 it was a popular spot to watch cricket.

Its popularity continued into this century and one woman still remembers the area in the 1920's: "People used to come out from Bristol to the river and Frenchay Common, especially on Good Friday and at Easter. The common would be thick with people. They went to Bullocks Tea Gardens down by the River Frome by the bridge just off Pearce's Hill. Another big attraction was the cricket. They played on the pitch facing the west end of the church. Nobody was allowed to go anywhere near the wicket and people accepted rules like that. These days they would trample all over it.

"There were many events on the common. Sometimes there would be a fair with small hand roundabouts and swings for the children. Before the First World War, there would be bands playing in the evening and the older people would dance. Frenchay stayed very rural for many years with no electricity in the village until the early 1930's. Paraffin lamps were hung up to provide light and cooking was over stoves and ranges. The farmer from a farm off Quarry Road went round with a horse and cart delivering milk. There was no rubbish collected and we used to dump it in a quarry hole up near the common.

"There was no piped water in the area, but there were plenty of springs and I remember, as a child, being sent for water from a beautiful spring off Chapel Lane. There was a gate at the top and you had to get a key to go in. I used to have to go there if my mother wanted to set a jelly as it had really cold water. Eventually the water authority said the spring water wasn't fit to drink."

It was a lad from Downend, who used to attract the attention of the cricketing fans to Frenchay on hot summer days in the Victorian era. William Gilbert Grace, better known as "WG" was born in Downend on July 18, 1848. A doctor's son, his cricketing prowess became legendary and he soon entered first class cricket and became captain of Gloucestershire. His massive frame and black beard dominated every game in which he played and some of his first exploits were on that precious wicket facing Frenchay church.

Community spirit in Yesterday's Island: 1935 jubilee celebrations, Grafton Street, St. Philips's Marsh.

In 50 years playing he scored over 50,000 runs, and took over 2,800 wickets. His highest batting score ever was 344. He died on October 23, 1915 but his name remains as a legend in both the sport and in the area in which he was born.

One area of East Bristol has sadly disappeared as a community but its spirit lives on—perhaps stronger than ever. It is the "island" of St Philips.

Of course, St Philips Marsh is not an island in the proper sense of the word but it was a thriving community that grew up on the piece of land bordered by the Feeder Canal on one side and the Avon on the other. More than 6,000 people lived on that tiny patch of ground. Despite poverty, or perhaps because of it, they developed a very strong community spirit. During the 1980's that spirit has been revived with a play, *Yesterday's Island*, and books and memoirs of the area.

The Marsh developed as industry came to East Bristol after the digging of the canal, and in 1874 St Silas church was opened and became the focal point for the whole area.

Loyalty to each other and to the church, school, chapel and local club were the hallmarks of an area that comprised just over 20 streets, each with its own general store.

But rats and mice abounded, amongst the dirt and grime of industry and the Marsh chimney-sweep, Mr A Gillett, added vermin catching to his list of activities. Another well-known local character was Gran Simmons, who lived in Grafton Street and who was known to everyone as Maggie.

Perhaps the spirit of the Marsh is best summed up in the motto printed on the front cover of every edition of the St Silas School magazine in the 1920's. It said: "St Silas, St Silas, For Honour, For Loyalty, For Courage, For Courtesy, Play Up, Play Fair, Play the Game."

St Silas parish hall, later known as Grafton Hall, became a hive of activity every day. During the depression of the 1930's the area suffered some of the worst poverty in Bristol but that only emphasised the closeness of the community. In 1941 incendiary bombs fell on the church. The call went out to the community and, within four days, a temporary church had been made ready, with ornaments, fabrics and furniture rescued from the blaze.

The school closed in 1958 due to falling numbers and gradually families moved out of the area. Now only the Dogs' Home, opened in 1901, and still functioning today, remains to show how the community once cared. The 1920's have been beautifully documented by the residents themselves and no brief history could do them justice.

Entertainment centred on a piece of arable land, formerly known as the Bean Field and later named Sparke Evans Park. This was a public pleasure ground with swimming baths and football pitches. It was also the scene of the sports day and fêtes, and the ultimate destination of the Queen of the Marsh parade, which assembled in St Silas and wound its way through Albert Crescent. The death knell came when the council designated St Philips as an industrial area, and used compulsory purchase orders to move out the last of the tenants.

Entertainment in East Bristol was never in short supply for those who were willing to go out and find it. One older Eastville resident remembers: "When we were youngsters we used to go up around the coal pit at Speedwell. When it was closed it was an ideal place for kids with bikes. Another popular jaunt was a walk through Eastville Park and out into the country. We used to walk along, following the river, and at the far end there was an open air swimming pool. It soon became derelict and was hardly ever used.

"There were also Fishponds Lido. That has got smaller and smaller over the years as houses have gradually been built on the land around. We were told that the water was so deep that if you fell in they would never find your body. I think that a lot of those tales were from people trying to frighten us off going near the water. Another popular outing for us kids was on Saturday morning when there was a 2d rush at the Vandyke. In the afternoon there was a 3d matinee at His Majesty's in Eastville and you got better films there."

Another popular attraction was the Eastville Pool, which was built in 1905 by Messrs J Perkins at a cost of £2,320 as part of a nationwide chain designed to combat respiratory diseases. In its heyday hundreds of people must have learned to swim safely in its patrolled waters.

Attendants were paid 25s each per week and 2s 6d on Sundays. Men and boys were allowed to swim for 1d and a towel cost an extra 1d. There was one strong rule: "Boys over 14 required to wear drawers".

In the winter of 1939 the pool was used as a water tank on standby in case it was needed for wartime fire-fighting duties. Perhaps the Germans knew of its strategic use for at 7pm on November 24, 1940, bombs dropped on Eastville. Four people were killed in Eastville Park and a stick of bombs fell across the area. The lining of the pool was irreparably damaged. It remained derelict for 40 years until recently when work began to turn it into a garden and recreation area.

Included in the project is a space for dramatic performances and there have certainly been a large number of those throughout East Bristol over the years. One elderly woman remembered the Barton Hill Mummers performing between 1900 and 1910. They traditionally gave their performance on Boxing Day. Many of the mummers were dustmen and they performed with their faces blacked, wearing paper frills, ribbons and odd attire and carrying banjos and concertinas.

The St George Mummers used to simply push open cottage doors and leap uninvited into people's living rooms. Their style consisted of marching around the table, which they would strike with their wooden swords before starting their verses.

The Kingswood Mummers were all tall men, who wore tall hats. Most of them belonged to one family and they carried bells and short steel swords. Each group stuck firmly to the mummery of tradition with St George, Father Christmas, the King of Egypt, the Turkish Knight, the Doctor and Punchinello as the main characters. Sometimes the words and rhymes were changed to make them more topical.

The face of East Bristol changed once again between the First and Second World Wars with the great council housing boom. People were moved out of slums in the central areas of Bristol and some were found new homes on the eastern fringe of the city. This new building destroyed more of the fields and created new suburbs.

A council housing estate of 1,544 homes on 180 acres was built in Fishponds in just 10 years, with work beginning in June 1920 and being completed by June 1930. Another 866 houses were built at St George between July 1924 and March 1931. The Hillfields estate was one of the first started after the First World War and half the houses were parlour type, which meant they had two rooms downstairs.

The area was changing in many other ways. Those electric trams, which had been greeted with such enthusiasm, bowed out with an equally uproarious farewell. Saturday, September 3, 1938 saw the last electric tram on the Old Market to Staple Hill line. Souvenir hunters stripped some of the trams on their farewell run so badly that one had to be steered with a spanner and ten had to be towed in because they had been wrecked.

At Staple Hill, one tram reached the Gloucestershire boundary at Cassell Road and an official of Mangotsfield urban district council carried out a closing ceremony before two horses were attached to the front of the tram to pull it the last mile home to the terminus.

Some carried on into wartime but the Good Friday Blitz of April 11, 1941 marked the end of the road. The last evening cars from Old Market to Kingswood and from Hanham to St George were on their way as enemy bombers flew overhead. The crews were pleased to be heading away from the city centre.

The Kingswood tram had reached Regent Street when the power went off—it had been cut by a bomb falling on St Philip's Bridge. The driver and conductor gave the tram a push and it was sent sailing down the last hill into the depot. It soon became clear that the power would not be restored as the damage was so bad and buses replaced the final trams.

The bombs falling in the Second World War in some ways finished a job in the inner city which the authorities had already started. As early as 1922, housing committee minutes were already recording the poor conditions into which properties had fallen. A demolition order was made on houses in Berkeley Street, Eastville because the owners had not carried out repairs. Three houses in Australian Place, Easton, were ordered to be demolished; a cottage at Stapleton was in a bad state of repair, and Pitt View Cottages, East Bristol, were in danger from a coal tip. In 1923 the committee minutes show that houses in Whitehall Road and Victoria Road were in poor condition and Dibbles Court, St Philips was branded as unfit for habitation.

Great Western Lane in Barton Hill was demolished and the new Housing Acts gave the council powers to clear the unhealthy areas. With the buildings and houses went the local communities.

The Great Western Cotton factory, which had supplied so much employment, was sold in January 1926 and became the Viscose Silk Company. The building went for £80,000 and the new company tried to keep work going with the production of artificial silk. But the experiment never worked and the factory closed in December 1929. It was later used as a warehouse.

East Bristol was slowly, for better or for worse, being dragged into the twentieth century. The progress reached dizzy heights in 1958 when the 15-storey high Barton House was completed. The tower block was the first of its kind in the country outside London and it was named after the area which had been destroyed to build it—Barton Hill. At the opening ceremony it was said: "The new Barton Hill will be worthy of the men, women and children who will come and live here in the future."

Councillors and council officers gathered on the roof of the tower block and said they were pioneering a housing revolution for the rest of the country to follow. The flats were described as: "clean, airy, well-serviced with magnificent views, communal facilities and all mod cons." Now, of course, views about tower blocks have changed with particular concern for children living in them.

Besides modern housing the new world needed bigger, wider and faster roads to get the new cars from place to place. Road widening and new road building has destroyed and split up many of the older areas of East Bristol.

Easton was described as "a storm centre of compulsory purchase" during the sixties as the council carried out an "experimental" method of redevelopment. By 1966 it was little but a wasteland with odd pockets of old houses and old businesses trying to get a living in the middle of the rubble. A 17-storey skyscraper under construction dominated the scene.

Len Williams, landlord of the Cornish Mount in Pennywell Road told the *Evening Post* at that time: "Tuesdays and Wednesdays you could say it is really dead. It is hardly worthwhile putting the heat and lights on.

"But they still come back at weekends. They were all brought up together and this is still their local where they come to meet one another, no matter how far away they have been moved."

The Minister for Housing, Richard Crossman, saw the area differently. He laid a foundation stone at one block of flats and said this sort of clearing and re-building of an area should be copied elsewhere.

In the seventies came the Outer Circuit Road, which split the area. In 1972 the people living in Twinnell House complained about the new road. One said: "The road is a monster, tearing the heart out of our community. Totterdown and Bedminster will be next unless we raise a protest. I hope that people will take a lesson from what is happening here and halt the road."

Those complaints marked the changes that ended the old style of living. Today's modern houses and roads generated a new type of community with its own characters and its own problems.

Yet much remains from the past. The tram lines have gone and so have the gas lights. But on those two main routes out of Bristol there are still reminders of the intrepid travellers who marked out these routes centuries ago.

From Bemmy Down to Bishopsworth

Martin J Powell tells how South Bristol exchanged slums for housing estates and found a new community spirit.

"A tortuous, grimy street is the main thoroughfare of Bedminster. Medieval gabled houses, sheds and tan pits drag their unsightly lengths from the rickety bridge which spans the Cut to the pretentiously named, but antiquated hostelry known as the London Inn."

That extract from the *South Bristol Gazette* of 1864 graphically describes Bedminster—the gateway to South Bristol. Cynics may say that little has changed, give or take a few medieval gabled houses. But in the last 100 years South Bristol has developed into a strange mixture of industry, council estates and private housing all nestling together. That "tortuous grimy street" still remains as East Street, the main shopping area, despite many modern superstores on the estates.

If you had passed through it 100 years ago you would soon have been in the countryside. Areas like Ashton, Hartcliffe, Withywood, Knowle and Brislington were largely fields, with farming the main work. But you would also have come across tough mining folk working the hard Bedminster and Ashton Vale coal field. There were frequent fights on Bedminster Down between the "Bemmy Down Blinders"—hard coal miners who worked and played with grim enthusiasm. Between 1840 and 1880 there were 21 mines in the area.

By 1887 only five mines were being worked and the last pit in South Liberty Lane closed down in 1924. Work, and thankfully working conditions, were changing from the traditional industries of farming and mining to the modern factories—mainly tobacco and the inter-related packaging industry.

South Bristol was gradually being dragged into the sprawl of the city, but those tough miners and farm workers certainly didn't go down without a fight. Their opposition to becoming part of Bristol is graphically illustrated by what went on in Brislington and Bishopsworth, quite separately, at that time.

Brislington was then described as "one of the prettiest villages in the whole of Somerset" and most of the land was owned by the Clayfield-Irelands and the Cooke-Hurles, rich local gentry. In this rural atmosphere the vestry committee ran local affairs at their meetings, presided over by the vicar.

In March 1891 the villagers faced the threat of being included within the Bristol boundary and local worthies gathered at the Assembly Rooms—now the Christadelphian Hall in Church Hill.

The chairman was the local vicar, Alfred Richardson, and the group was in an angry mood. They drew up a document to make their case to Somerset county council, a plea not to be included in the City of Bristol. The village, they insisted, "neither requests nor desires the urban benefits which would result from inclusion in the City of Bristol."

The county council was told that Brislington, 1,180 acres of land and 240 houses, was "not of an urban character." The population of the village had only grown by four in the previous 10 years, rising from 1,717 in 1881 to 1,721 in 1891. And knowing that then, as now, money was the most important thing to councils, Somerset was told that it would lose income of £160 a year if it allowed the village to go.

Fowler's Local Government Act of 1894 established parish councils, and in Bishopsworth the parish of Bedminster Without was formed. "Without what?" was the popular question of the day. "Without the city, of course", locals proudly answered.

But that same council had to draw up battle plans when Knowle and Totterdown were swallowed up by the city under the Bristol Boundaries Bill. Along with the age-old row over the level of rates, the fight against Bristol was one of the recurring items on the parish agenda. But in 1906 the parish had reason to regret the battle when the Bishopsworth village pub, The Elm Tree Inn, burned down. A message was sent to the Bristol Fire Brigade which refused to come as it had no jurisdiction outside the city boundary. It is doubtful if the firemen would have saved the day anyway as their horse-drawn tender would have had to negotiate Bedminster Down Hill before reaching the blaze. Locals did what they could with buckets of water, while miners shouted at them to throw the water at the slate so that their debts were erased!

Within a year later, the village spent £37 10s to form its own fire brigade.

The shows of independence worked for a remarkably long time, as Brislington did not come into the city boundary until 1933 and Bishopsworth held out until 1956. That fierce independence, spawned in those days of horse-drawn fire tenders and vestry committees, is what binds together most of the differing areas of South Bristol today.

The Victorian urge to build gradually changed the area. Rural Brislington started to disappear in 1878 when the Bellvue Park area was built in a small T-shape of roads. Builder William Vowles put up those houses because there was not enough room for the workers on the estates to live. Miners' cottages and Victorian villas began to spring up in Bedminster, slowly encroaching on the fields.

The St Anne's area was closer to the city and when in 1892 the local landowner, George Sinnott of Langton Court, died, it became

Bedminster from the air, 1928.

clear it would become built up. Langton Road, as it is now, was one of the first to be built. But it was originally called The Drive, as it was on the driveway to Langton Court.

But these small building projects going on throughout the area were nothing compared to what was to come.

There was a problem in Bedminster. Outside the city the farm workers and labourers could cope with their simple village life; the miners, though rough and hard, could eke out a reasonable living. But as the 20th century got under way, there was increasing pressure to do something about the slums in which city dwellers were living around Bedminster.

Bedminster had a smoky atmosphere, which came from the houses and factories. Tall chimneys were everywhere by the 1920's. Smoke belched forth from the Ochre works, Wills, Robinson, Capper Pass, The Malthouse, tanneries, glue works and railway engines.

Many of the poorest people lived in the middle of the smoke and grime of industry, in cobbled courts which opened out into little communities with half a dozen houses in each. Large council estates were to be built in South Bristol during the 1930's to rehouse the families that lived in these places.

One man, who lived in Stillhouse Lane, Bedminster, remembers the conditions well. "When I look at the area now it seems impossible that so many people lived in such a small space," he said. "We were a fairly typical family with mother and father, three girls and two boys. There were also two other boy babies that died while we were in that house.

"We shared a house in Stillhouse Lane with another family—there were eight of them. The house had just two bedrooms and we paid 3s of the 6s 6d a week rent. Seven of us slept in one bedroom. At first we children all slept in the same bed with girls' heads up one end and boys at the other. I would sleep with my sisters' feet on either side of my head. Old overcoats were thrown over us as bedclothes. We didn't really think about the conditions at the time but they were filthy by today's standards. We used to pull open the seams on the overcoats over us and find fleas inside to kill—we did that just for something to do.

"My grandmother and grandfather lived nearby in Squire's Court and 30 people lived there in six houses. There must have been hundreds of people living in the little courts that ran throughout the area."

Sanitation in the house in Stillhouse Lane consisted of a tap and sink outside in a back yard. Nearby were two toilets that flushed by sluicing a bucket of water down them.

"My father was a casual docker, which meant that he went every morning to the docks and was taken on only if there was work for him," he recalled. "We lived by getting things from the local corner

Weaver's Buildings, Bedminster. Demolished in slum clearance, 1933.

shops where they knew us and would let us have things 'on trust' if no money was available. We ate mostly stews and any kind of meat or offal we could get. My mother said she could feed all of us and my grandparents for a shilling. A stew would consist of 1lb of 'cutting', which were meat scraps that cost 4d; 2lbs of 'all sorts', which was usually a carrot, a turnip and an onion and cost 2d, and 5lb of potatoes, which cost 3d.

"Often if we had money I would be sent to the shops with that list. The other frequent visit was to the pawn shops in Bedminster with a bundle of clothes. Long queues could always be seen outside the pawn shop on a Monday morning. We usually pawned a bundle for 2s 6d but always asked for 3s as the man behind the counter would knock you down 6d.

"I can remember a row once when my sister's engagement ring was pawned. If my father didn't come home by 10 o'clock we knew he had got work so the ring went to the pawn shop and then I was sent to get a sub off him to get the ring back out before my sister came home and found out what had happened."

Few of the people living in the courts and roads around bought things from the busy shopping street of Bedminster. They were known in the local corner shops, which sold everything they might need. There were also frequent street traders who would visit the area selling their wares.

"The one I most remember is the fly paper man. He wore a top hat and he would shout: "Catch 'em alive—Oh those tormenting flies". Kids would chase him up the streets. Most people had fly papers covered in flies hanging in their houses. There were also people selling cockles and fruit.

"Entertainment also came down the street with a hurdy-gurdy man about once a week. They would do a turn in the street, sometimes doing cartwheels all down the street. I don't know how they lived as few people gave them money. They used to get the odd ha'penny and that must have been enough to keep them in food."

One of the most famous courts in the area developed its own industry as a key to survival, and was nicknamed "Stickchopper's Court". About once a week all the residents of the court would gather in the central area. They would collect packing cases or anything made of wood during the week and would chop it up to make bundles of firewood. Each bundle would be tied with a thread pulled from a sack. These were sold to the local shops, who would sell it on as firewood. The court then shared out the profit among themselves.

With everyone cooking over open fires, the wood was an essential that most people had to buy. In Stillhouse Lane, children would often gather around piles of waste material put outside by businesses that had furnaces. Quite young children were experts at spotting bits that had not been burned fully and that could be used on the family fire for cooking.

Industrial properties were side by side with houses. Carts loaded with dead animals would be brought through the streets to the glue factories and sometimes live animals were brought through the streets for slaughter. Rats were often seen. A new sport of jabbing bugs in the wall with pins was popular and cockroaches "of all the colours of the rainbow" came out at night according to those who lived there.

By 1919 the Government had passed a housing subsidy act to encourage local authorities to clear such slums and build new council housing estates. More acts of parliament followed in 1923, 1924, 1930, 1933 and 1935 and these were to transform South Bristol and create whole new suburbs of the city.

The 1919 houses were mostly built around St John's Lane, Bedminster with a few in Knowle. A non-parlour house cost £986 to build at this time, but became cheaper by the middle 1930's. In that time, before the Second World War, Bristol Corporation built nine housing estates throughout Bristol, and by far the largest was the Knowle and Bedminster Estate with 6,034 houses. The people living in the poor houses in Bedminster and in the courts were re-housed in the new estates, and their homes knocked down.

In Stillhouse Lane one resident remembers the house next door being knocked down: "The people next door were moved before us and when they knocked that house down cracks appeared in our bedroom ceiling and wall. We could see the stars and moon through them."

The family in that house was moved to Marksbury Road in Bedminster. Suddenly the one family had three bedrooms, a gas cooker, a bath and a boiler that enabled them to pump hot water into the bathroom. "It was sheer luxury. My mother used to put newspapers down on the floor because she didn't want us to get the floor dirty. But the move meant that we lost touch with most of the people that we knew as they were moved to different places."

The council house building in South Bristol swallowed up acres of countryside and changed the face of the entire area in just 20 years.

On Bedminster Down building work started in October 1925. By September 1929 442 new houses had been built on 53 acres of fields and a population of 2,281 had grown there by 1939. In St Anne's, 45 acres of land were used to build 462 houses between February 1928 and September 1933. By the outbreak of war there were 2,313 people living in those new homes.

The Knowle and Bedminster estate saw a staggering 1,044 acres swallowed up by 6,034 houses to make homes for 27,644 people by 1939.

But beneath the bare statistics the estates were changing people's lives to an incredible degree. Many resented the new housing conditions or felt they could not change their way of life sufficiently to cope. The Knowle and Bedminster estate was so big that it formed a perfect cross-section of all the types of houses and people moved into them during those Government Acts aimed at improving housing. From East to West the estate fell into three main social zones.

At Knowle Park were the expensive 1919 and 1923 Act houses and the more prosperous tenants. Next was a wide band of houses built under the 1924 Wheatley Act, which had lower rents. Knowle West at the western end had most of the slum-clearance houses built under the 1930 Act to which families from the oldest and worst slum areas were moved. Finally at the extreme western end of the estate, later houses were built for those living in overcrowded conditions.

Knowle West with most of the slum clearance families rapidly got a reputation for being rough and unpleasant. The council had thought little about the social effects of shunting people into new houses, and was surprised to find that instead of becoming middle-class people with pride in their homes, they simply carried on in their old ways. By 1935, the reputation had grown so bad that some other families were refusing to move into the area. The council realised that they had simply built a wilderness of houses and action must be taken to give the area some heart.

Plans for a municipal social centre were drawn up and for the equivalent of a market town High Street, so that people could get their shopping locally. The street, Filwood Broadway, was designed to contain several shops and multiple stores, as well as a cinema. It was never completed to its full design because the war intervened. The social centre was opened in May 1938 in a quadrangle and is still the social centre of the area today.

The occasion of the opening of the centre was used to re-name the district Filwood Park as a way of combatting the Knowle West stigma. But the old name has never died out and people in the area still prefer to proudly call themselves Knowle Westers.

Filwood Social Centre included rooms which voluntary associations could hire; a hall with dance floor and stage; a gymnasium, canteen, meeting-rooms, skittle alley, workshop and reading room. One side of the quadrangle of buildings was designed for use by adults and the opposite side for juveniles, with the hall and gymnasium completing the square. But the authorities frowned on pubs as they felt these might encourage drunkeness on the estates. It was the late 30's before the Venture Inn was built in Knowle and 1945 before the area got a second pub.

Most of the houses on the estates were parlour-type with two rooms downstairs. A survey carried out in the 1940's described the

Top: An off-duty shift at the Capper Pass smelting works in 1887. **Bottom:** hand-rolling cigars at Wills in the 1940s.

houses built in Bristol South like this: "All the council houses included a bathroom and WC either upstairs or downstairs (the latter is generally preferred by large families), a larder and a coal shed as well as a scullery for cooking and washing.

"The living-room, which is fairly large in non-parlour houses, has to be used as a nursery, as well as for eating and sitting. In houses with a parlour, the living-room is smaller than in non-parlour houses, but the bedrooms are larger.

"One cupboard and a large dresser for crockery are provided in the living-room; there is a cupboard under the stairs. Upstairs on the landing there is a small linen store; there is generally a built-in cupboard in one bedroom. The downstairs rooms and two main bedrooms contain open fire grates. In the great majority of cases gas is used for cooking and for the wash-boiler. Normally, bath water is heated in the copper and pumped to the bathroom by hand, but some tenants instal geysers. There is no constant hot water system and no hand basin in the bathroom."

But despite these new-found luxuries, many of the new inhabitants of the estates complained that they were like barracks and that they were too far away from shopping centres like Bedminster. There was also rivalry between different parts of the Knowle estate as older residents resented the newcomers from the slums moving in to their area. Surveys carried out by the city council and Bristol University at the time revealed "a sense of restlessness and frustration" in parts of the new estate as people felt they had been shoved into artificial new conditions with no community spirit to bind them.

Many of the men in the slums were on casual work—15 per cent on the new estates earned their living this way. It was harder for these men now they were further away from the city centre and the docks.

People who had previously lived by such things as hawking for furniture removal work in the central area now found it impossible on the outskirts of the city and the resentment built up.

A new trend developed for bicycles. Men who found it difficult to walk into the centre of Bristol every day for work began to cycle in from Knowle and Bedminster. Many others used the bus. The bus company introduced a "workman's ticket" to get people to the centre of the city for work at a cheaper rate. The rate was so attractive that housewives at Knowle West got up and were waiting on the bus stops before 8am so that they could take advantage of the reduced fares to the cheaper shops in East Street, Bedminster.

By the 1940's in Filwood Park, there were 17 shops in Melvin Square, Leinster Avenue, Newquay Road and Filwood Broadway. They included two Co-operative Stores, each with several departments, and a few that sold just about everything that you could want.

For a number of years, the only meat available on the estate came from the Co-operative Stores in Melvin Square and one other butcher in Newquay Road. The stock kept by them was limited and many of the cheap cuts and offal available in East Street could not be got on the new estate. So most of the shoppers still went to Bedminster for their meat. Until just before the war it was impossible to buy hardware and clothes on the new estate. It was a stark contrast to the bustling street scenes of Bedminster, where most of the occupants had previously lived.

But wherever there is a shortage there is always someone ready to step into the breach, and roundsmen soon flourished on the Knowle and Bedminster estate. Fish, fruit, vegetables, sweets, magazines, clothes, hardware, cockles and toy balloons were rapidly available in the streets or from door to door. There was also a fish and chip van making two rounds of the estate a day.

But to live properly, most families had to go to Bedminster to do their shopping at least once a week. So the tradition of a Friday or Saturday visit to East Street was formed. The return fare from Filwood park to Mill Lane, Bedminster was 3d, and the cost was easily made up by buying in Bedminster. Some things like pigs trotters, chitterling and pig's cheek were cheaper than any meat that could be bought in Filwood. A small packet of Persil was 3d in Bedminster, a halfpenny cheaper than on the estate; a packet of Rinso was 5½d instead of 6d and sugar was 5½d for 2lbs instead of 6d.

But simply moving people to the suburbs did not end the poverty and a survey in 1939 showed that half the children in Knowle West were living below the poverty line. A social worker, who lived on the estate for several months that year wrote: "The distress of the Knowle Bedminster estate is hidden when the inhabitants are indoors, but is pathetically, almost ironically, obvious when they are out and about and thrown up against the background of the bright new homes.

"There is no doubt that living on the estates in many cases leads to an improvement in health. Nevertheless, many children show pathetic traces of lack of sleep and proper food. Child pneumonia and adult asthma are still far too prevalent. It is astonishing to find the smallest children playing and singing in the street until well after ten on summer evenings. The lack of a resident doctor leads to delays in dealing with urgent cases of illness.

"Most families appear reasonably contented with their new houses and would not wish to return to the centre, not at any rate into their previous homes. Some are very happy. Even those parents who cannot themselves get used to the estates are reconciled to them for the sake of their children.

"The houses are greatly appreciated. Most tenants enjoy their

Top: Totterdown: a thriving community until the traffic planners moved in during the 1960s. It was twenty years before houses were being built here again. **Bottom:** Sandy Park, Brislington.

114

gardens, with the exception of families whose men do heavy manual work. The great majority of gardens admirably reflect the care taken of them; when the lack of experience in gardening and means to buy tools are remembered, the results achieved are still more impressive."

But perhaps the over-riding feeling for many of the new residents was how quiet the area was after their previous homes. At the time they were built, they were right on the edge of the city so there was no through traffic. In Bedminster and the centre of the city the people had been used to living side by side with industry. The residential streets of Knowle had no factory noises, and in 1932, when the first tenants moved in, they complained that they had been banished to a strange, quiet, treeless plateau on the outskirts of the city.

But the council were not the only people building houses and developing the suburbs of South Bristol in the 1930's. A thriving market existed for private houses for those with more money.

Attractive bay window houses had existed at the same time as the slums of Bedminster, in Windmill Hill, Southville, St John's Lane, The Chessels, Lower Knowle and Totterdown. These had been built in the late Victorian era and formed estates for the better-off with regular work in the area. In 1932, a house in St John's Lane, Bedminster could be secured for just £25 deposit.

The growth of private ownership in South Bristol led to the Bristol and West Building Society opening their first branch office in Cannon Street, Bedminster in 1931. Under the slogan: "They are wise who invest in the Bristol and West", the office did brisk business, and a queue of the better-off Bedminster residents could be seen outside when mortgage payment day came around.

The private house-builders were not only putting up small developments. The whole area of Headley Park was constructed on 60 acres of land overlooking the valley of the Malago stream. In 1934 and 1935 a house on the Headley Park estate was selling for £360. Buyers had to put down a deposit of £25 and then pay just over 9s a week.

The 60 acres were originally Headley Farm and were bought by the Bristol Development and Construction Company, which had been searching for some time for a pleasant area in which to build houses cheaply. Three styles of houses were built, costing £360, £385 and £435. Each had an entrance hall, living room, kitchen, larder, cupboard, bath and lavatory, and three bedrooms. The roads were built in curves and loops off a main estate road, which was originally going to be called St Michael's Rise, but was eventually called St Peter's Rise.

The hilly area on the edge of Bristol seemed to be miles away to some city dwellers so the sellers went to great lengths to point out that it was just 1½ miles from East Street and 2¼ miles from Bristol Bridge.

A chirpy chap called Jack featured in the *Western Daily Press* advertisements for the estate. He described the site like this:

"Twenty acres have been planned as open spaces. Furthermore there are a lot of trees knocking about and the roads and houses have been planned so that these trees will remain. And is it healthy up there? Do you know the estate is 200 feet above sea level. What a breeze there was tonight. It sweeps over Dundry from the Mendips like-well like the zephyr and something or other, and the scenery is fine. On the south side you have a gorgeous sweep of the country around Dundry, and over to the west is a fine stretch of meadowland over Whitchurch way."

The "fine stretch of meadowland" is now taken up partly by W D and H O Wills' tobacco factory, but who could resist a house in such an alpine location!

Buyers were also attracted by the services planned for the new estate. A bus service was promised every 15 minutes, and an open air swimming pool, cinema and hotel were scheduled in the future. The Second World War stopped these plans.

The Redcliffe Furnishing Company offered £5 worth of furniture free to anyone who bought a house on the estate. The value of this offer can be fully appreciated when it is realised that the company completely furnished the show house on the site for just £45. Loans for first-time buyers could be arranged with the Liverpool Investment Building Society, to be paid off in 23 years.

Many of the houses today on the estate will have lost some of the features that attracted the original owners. In the bathroom a geyser "of the modern type, chromium plated and white enamelled" provided the hot water. Advertisements for the estate also said: "Purchasers are invited to choose wallpapers for the sitting room up to 1s 9d a piece; hall, landing and bedroom up to 1s 6d a piece; and borders in the sitting room and bedrooms up to 4d a yard."

Today with its own school and shops the estate is as established in South Bristol as any of the older areas.

Members of the B Company of the 6th Gloucestershire Regiment had practised trench digging by excavating the foundations for Headley Park and they soon had to put that new skill to use. The war stopped the expansion of South Bristol for a time as people concentrated on the war effort, with cigarettes for the forces being produced in W D and H O Wills, Bedminster.

Many of the gardens were provided with Anderson Shelters. Some of these shelters are in use to this day in the area. Now above ground, they form useful corrugated metal garden sheds.

Many homes were destroyed in the area in the German bombing raids, but the worst night for South Bristol, and particularly

Top: Coronation party, Catherine Mead Street, Bedminster, 1953. **Bottom:** Gilbert Street, Ashton Gate when the fate of these houses was in the balance in the late 1950s.

Bedminster, was Friday, April 11, 1941—Good Friday.

The war ended with a wave of street parties, and a baby-boom which created a whole new problem for the authorities. The housing waiting list had grown longer and Bristol still had many of its pre-war slums. The biggest drive yet to build new houses was soon underway, and in 1955 Bristol Corporation was building a staggering 50 houses a week.

Soon after the war surveyors were seen looking over the fields between Knowle and the slopes of Dundry, seeking land on which to build massive new housing estates. The pressures from the slums; the shortage of housing following the war and the baby-boom meant that things had to be done fast. Imaginative schemes were dreamed up to create a beautiful estate in South Bristol, but these were rejected in favour of the cheapest and the simplest. Bristol housing committee decided to name the massive new estate after the old Hundred of Hartcliffe.

Massive it certainly was. By the time the houses were finished the estate had as many residents as the ancient town of Chichester. But the need to build quickly meant that once again city people had been shunted into the suburbs with little thought for facilities.

The first impressions of the early residents in Hartcliffe were not encouraging. People moving in during the early 1950's found no proper streets or pavements; just one road through the estate and a little piece of concrete at the front door. The rest was a sea of mud. The building work had been done so quickly that many residents were moving in before the paint was dry. For seven years there was no pub and church congregations met wherever they could, as no church buildings had been provided. Some tradesmen refused to deliver because the roads on the new estate were so muddy and incomplete, and Hartcliffe people went to collect coal in prams.

But the residents were grateful for the new-style houses and a unique community spirit soon emerged, unmatched in the rest of the city. From 1954 to 1959 the community association met in White-house School, the first to be built in Hartcliffe. Activities began to raise funds for a community centre. People collected money door-to-door, a barrel organ went around the streets and many events were held. In 1958, community leaders organised an outing to Weymouth, and twelve coaches took 600 people on the day trip at a cost of 7s 6d each. That community spirit grew up from the very first meetings of residents in a builders' hut on the estate.

As soon as new buildings went up they were put to use by the community. Whitehouse Junior School was used by mothers for handicraft sessions even before it was officially opened. A baby clinic was also started in the Congregational Church Hall.

Perhaps the highlight for the new estate came in 1957 when Princess Margaret visited the area to meet residents coping with

Bristol Airport, Whitchurch.

the alien atmosphere of a modern council estate. The Princess wore a shimmering silver grey outfit and her visit took a very informal form.

She was welcomed to Hareclive School, where she met pupils and then she strolled up the flower-lined garden path of St Andrew's vicarage to share a meal with the vicar's wife, Mrs Ronald Armstrong. Mrs Armstrong had spent the morning preparing tomato soup, Severn salmon and a sweet for the Princess. Then the Princess chatted to families in Millard House and looked around their homes. It was the perfect tonic for the estate, which had suffered a bad reputation through vandalism. Many of the young people on the estate with nothing to do had turned to causing damage as a way to vent their frustration. But as more facilities were fought for with that same spirit that had kept the south of the area going for so many years, the estate soon developed a character of its own.

One thing that had been carefully researched in Hartcliffe was the street naming, and Bristol housing manager, Mr H C W Harris, had ensured that the streets had names of historical relevance to the area. Hareclive Road was named after the original form of the name Hartcliffe, (from hare, the Saxon word for army, and clive, meaning a steep rugged cliff). The name came from battles fought in the district in the time of the ancient Britons. Bishport Avenue comes from the original name for Bishopsworth, and Arundel Close from Thomas Arundel, former Lord of the Manor of Long Ashton.

Many of the other areas in South Bristol have historic street names or names picked as part of a theme. In Ashton, the Smyth family is remembered in names like Greville Road (after Greville Smyth). Themes for road names vary from precious stones in The Chessels (Pearl Street, Ruby Street and Jasper Street), to Somerset towns and villages in Bedminster Down (Cheddar Grove, Ilchester Crescent, Banwell Close).

One street, now in the centre of Bedminster, is called Mount Pleasant and marks the end of one of the earliest building booms. It was given the unusual name because at the time it was built, it had marvellous views across green fields. The St Anne's Park area was named after famous cathedrals with St David's Crescent, Rochester Road and Coventry Walk.

Brislington has changed from the quiet country village of a century ago to a bustling city suburb savagely split by a major four lane highway. Many of the older houses have long histories from the days when the village was strung out along the main Bath Road. In 1900, Brislington consisted of a Weslyan Methodist Chapel, the blacksmith's forge, four or five shops including the Post Office and a series of large houses, known by such names as Blagdon Lodge, Wisteria House, Homeside and The Hollies.

Hartcliffe in the making, 1957.

Brislington House was one of the first purpose built mental asylums in the country when Dr Edward Long Fox bought the land for £4,000 in 1799. Despite objections from the local church vestry, the doctor, who also ran a private asylum in Downend, built his house and ran it on humane grounds (for those days) even providing sporting facilities for the patients. Dr Fox was so well respected that he was once called to examine the mental state of George III. His skill is demonstrated in one story that he was grabbed by lunatics as he walked through the grounds and that they threatened to drown him in a bath. He escaped by persuading them to give three cheers before they killed him and the noise attracted the attention of attendants nearby. The patients were moved out in 1949 and the house is now a private nursing home.

The old and the new have now blended together perfectly in the suburbs of South Bristol so that many people cannot tell where one area begins and another ends.

The newer estates are now as well-established as the old country areas. Only the strange habit of people in places in Bishopsworth and Brislington of saying "down in the village" when they mean the local shops, gives away that still not forgotten time before they became a mere suburb of a city.

Acknowledgements

The following have been especially helpful in the compilation of this book:

Annals of Bristol by John Latimer

Bristol—An Architectural History by Andor Gomme, Michael Jenner, Bryan Little (Lund Humphries, 1979)

A Kingsdown Community by Penelope Mellor (published by the author, 1985)

Cotham Walks by Stephen Jones (Redland and Cotham Amenities Society, 1980)

Sneyd Park by Michael Morgan (published by the author, 1977)

Shirehampton Story by Ethel Thomas (published by the author, 1983)

Bristol Between the Wars ed David Harrison (Redcliffe Press, 1984)

Churches in Bristol by Bryan Little (Redcliffe Press, 1978)

Westbury Park Not So Long Ago by BDW (1983)

1250 Years at Westbury-on-Trym (Westbury-on-Trym Parish Church, 1967)

Walking Around Bristol by Helena Eason (Kingsmead, 1979)

St Judes Centenary 1949 (Church publication)

St Simon the Apostle 1847-1947 (Church publication)

Brookland Methodist Church Diamond Jubilee 1888-1948 (Church publication)

The writings of Max Barnes in the *Evening Post*.

Evening Post, Western Daily Press and the many Bristol newspapers which preceded or competed with them.

Malago Society

Bristol United Press library staff

Brislington Conservation and Amenity Society

The Government of Bristol 1373-1973 by Elizabeth Ralph

Bristol City Archives

Barton Hill History Society

Anton Bantock

Jonathan Rowe

Robert Powell

Gladys Harrison

Avon County Community Environmental Service (Acces)

Dennis Orchard

The Georgian Buildings of Bristol by Walter Ison

Tenants of Haberfield Almshouses, Hotwells

Clifton and Hotwells Improvement Society

Bristol University Extra Mural Local Studies Group

Alongside Bristol Quay by John Shaw (published by the author)

Many other Bristolians who gave freely of their time and memories.

Lesley Harrison for word processing, suggestions and support.

The Contributors

James Belsey, David Harrison, Martin J Powell and Pat Smith are all journalists on the *Evening Post*.

Helen Reid is a journalist on the *Western Daily Press*.

All the pictures in this book come from the Bristol United Press Archives which include many photographs inherited from newspapers like the *Bristol Times and Mirror*, *Bristol Evening News*, *Bristol Evening World*, the *Evening Times*, and *Bristol Observer*, none of which, sadly, has survived.

BRISTOL BOOKS

Redcliffe Press are the leading publishers of books about Bristol, having in the past ten years produced fifty on different aspects of the city's life and history. No other British city outside London has received such attention. This is both a measure of the richness and significance of Bristol's past and present, and of the intense pride and interest of Bristolians in their own city.

Redcliffe combines the very best in writing, research and illustration with high quality design and printing. The result is a wide and surprising range of books from 50 pence to £10, which are always tremendous value.

We are grateful to Bristol & West Building Society for joining us in a unique collaboration which, in addition to *Bristol: The Growing City*, has enabled publication of the following titles:

The Bristol Scene by Jennifer Gill £1.75

A fascinating glimpse of how the city looked in the early nineteenth century, just before the advent of the camera.

Many of the illustrations are from the priceless Braikenridge Collection in the City Art Gallery. George Weare Braikenridge, a retired merchant and plantation owner, had antiquarian interests, and commissioned nearly 1,500 drawings by local artists of Bristol between 1818 and 1830.

Victorian Buildings in Bristol by Clare Crick £2.25

The authoritative and highly acclaimed study of Bristol's great wealth of commercial, ecclesiastical, industrial and residential buildings from the nineteenth century. The author shows us masterpieces such as the 'Bristol Byzantine' Granary on Welsh Back and, by way of contrast, the sedate villas of Clifton, Cotham and Redland.

Changing Bristol by Tony Aldous £1.95

The author examines more than six dozen modern buildings and conservation schemes in the City of Bristol: some of national importance—Clifton Cathedral, the Bristol United Press building, W.D. & H.O. Wills at Hartcliffe and the High Kingsdown houses; imaginative conservation schemes such as Bush Warehouse and St Nicholas Church Museum, as well as the Ape House at Bristol Zoo.

Bedminster Between the Wars by Leonard Vear   £1.95

Published to mark the fiftieth anniversary of the Bristol & West's first branch office. It presents a fascinating picture of life in one of Bristol's best loved suburbs during the 1920s and 1930s.

Brunel's Bristol by Angus Buchanan and Michael Williams
Casebound £6.95   Paperbound £3.95

The first full study of the impact on Bristol of the celebrated Victorian engineer, with special reference to Clifton Suspension Bridge, SS Great Britain and Temple Meads Railway Station.

It tells of Brunel's triumphs, exasperations and disappointments in the city which, as a young man, he adopted as his own and which he continued to regard with affection for the rest of his life.

Bristol First by Bevan Rider   £1.75

Published to celebrate the bicentenary of the first ever mailcoach run, from Bristol to London on Monday August 2nd, 1784. This is the story of that historic journey told against the background of sustained political intriguing by opponents.

Bristol Glass ed. Cleo Witt   £7.95

A beautiful book about Bristol's glass industry from its heyday in the 18th century to the 1920s, when the city's last glass house went out of business. It features the famous 'Bristol Blue', and is a marvellous introduction to the important collection of glass in the City Museum and Art Gallery.

A smaller version, *Introducing Bristol Glass*, is also available paperbound at £2.25.

Redcliffe Press also publish books on a wide range of subjects, ranging from West Country to art, architecture, literature, biography and leisure interests.

For a complete catalogue, please write to us at 49, Park Street, Bristol 1 enclosing a s.a.e.